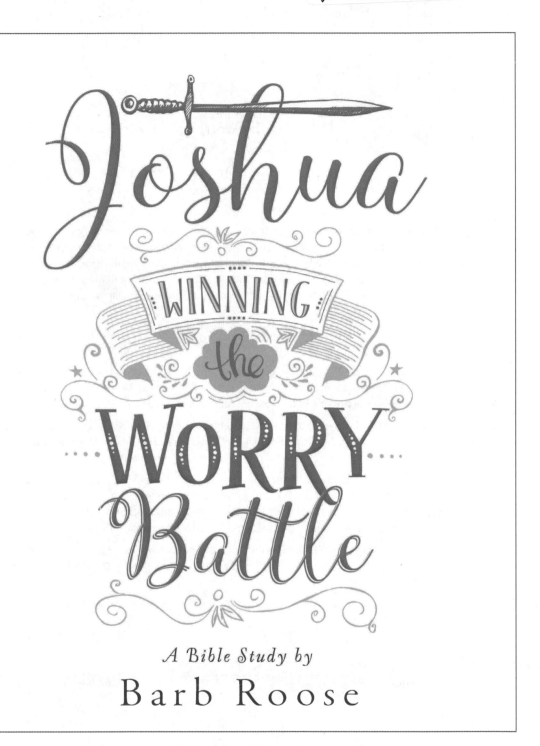

Joshua

WINNING *the* WORRY Battle

A Bible Study by

Barb Roose

Abingdon Women

Nashville

Joshua
Winning the Worry Battle

ISBN 978-1-5018-1360-3

20 21 22 23 24 25 26 27 — 10 9 8 7
MANUFACTURED IN THE UNITED STATES OF AMERICA

CONTENTS

ABOUT THE AUTHOR

Barb Roose is a popular speaker and author who is passionate about connecting women to one another and to God, helping them apply the truths of God's Word to the practical realities and challenges they face as women in today's culture. Barb enjoys teaching and encouraging women at conferences and events across the country, as well as internationally. She is the author of the *Joshua: Winning the Worry Battle* and *Beautiful Already: Reclaiming God's Perspective on Beauty* Bible studies and the books *Winning the Worry Battle: Life Lessons from the Book of Joshua* and *Enough Already: Winning Your Ugly Struggle with Beauty.* She also writes a regular blog at BarbRoose.com and hosts the "Better Together" podcast. Previously Barb was Executive Director of Ministry at CedarCreek Church in Perrysburg, Ohio, where she served on staff for fourteen years and co-led the annual Fabulous Women's Conference that reached more than ten thousand women over five years. Barb and her husband, Matt, live in Toledo, Ohio, and are the parents of three beautiful daughters.

Follow Barb:

  @barbroose

  @barbroose

  Facebook.com/barbararoose

Blog   BarbRoose.com
(check here for event dates and booking information)

INTRODUCTION TO THIS STUDY

Have you ever found yourself worrying about the bad things that could happen—whether they involve your family, your job, your finances, your health, or your future? Me, too! Have you ever spent a sleepless night worrying about the state of our nation or world? You aren't alone. If I had a dime for every time I've worried about something in my life, I might be tempted to start worrying about where to store all of those dimes!

As Christians, we know that we shouldn't worry, but the reality is that we all do at times. And when we try to fight worry with faith, often we feel that we're losing the battle. In those moments, well-intentioned comments like "God's got this!" or "Just pray about it" can leave us feeling even more burdened. Whether it's personal worries or broader concerns, we long for something more than clichés that will help us put real feet to our faith and win the worry battle.

There was a time in my life when I was losing the worry battle. In a fallen world filled with bad news, bad people, and bad decisions, worry felt like a handy strategy to keep me on my toes. I thought that if I could answer all of the "what if's," then maybe I could prevent some unknown inconvenience, pain, or tragedy in the future. (Have you ever felt that way?) Those "what if" questions popped up in every area of my life, and it seemed to make sense to try to find answers to them. Oh, the hours I spent thinking, rethinking, and overthinking all of the uncertainties in my life! What would happen if...

But then something changed.

What changed? Well, I wish that I could tell you that I prayed for God to take away my worry and, suddenly, it disappeared and never came back. That hasn't happened, but something even more amazing has! Over the years, God has equipped me to block, battle, and beat back worry from my life. Worry will always be a threat, but I'm not powerless against it. And neither are you! We can and must fight the worry battle, but we won't be able to win on our own. God will give us victory!

My worry battle is one of the reasons I was drawn to the Book of Joshua. Imagine the "what if" questions in the minds of millions of Israelites who'd traveled for many years to a place where they had never been before. They faced the kind of worries that you might be facing right now, such as what they would encounter next, where they would live, and how they would survive. They faced a battle not only with worry but also with very real enemies.

In this six-week study on the Book of Joshua, we will join God's people as they arrive in the hostile territory of Canaan and are surrounded by great uncertainty and formidable foes. Even though God gave the land to the Israelites over four hundred years before, they had to fight for and claim it. We'll see how God promised and paved the way to victory for His people when they showed up and fought in faith.

Along the way, we'll get to know the man Joshua, who led the Israelites in this fight. Joshua has been a hero of mine for many years, even inspiring me to jump out of an airplane (more about that later)! He almost seemed invincible to me; but as I studied how God communicated with Joshua, I realized that he likely fought his own worry battle. How encouraging it is to know that one of the Bible's most faithful heroes had to battle worry, too.

So, I invite you to join me on the battlefield as we learn to overcome a struggle that so many of us face each day. Whether you have worried, panicked, or even had a massive meltdown over friendship, family, financial, or future-related issues, God has a new path for you to follow. Joshua and the Israelites will show us the way, teaching us how to join forces with God and win over worry!

Getting Started

As we dig into the twenty-four chapters of the Book of Joshua, we will be exploring a six-step plan or approach for winning the worry battle, which involves 1) Facing Our Fears, 2) Letting God Fight for Us, 3) Getting into Position, 4) Attacking the Roots of Our Worries, 5) Receiving Our Victory, and 6) Living in Victory. Each week there are five readings or lessons combining study of Scripture with reflection and application. Space is provided for recording your responses and completing exercises. At the end of each day's lesson, you'll find one of five different "Apply It" experiences. They are titled according to the days of the week for some fun alliteration, but obviously you can do them on any day according to when you plan your study time:

- *Motivation Monday*: A motivating challenge for the day or week
- *Tool Tuesday*: A helpful tool to equip you to battle worry
- *Wisdom Wednesday*: An inspirational quote or verse
- *Temperature Check Thursday*: A time to reflect on how you are doing
- *Freedom Friday*: A prompt to celebrate how God has given you victory during your worry battle this week

Following this personal application, you'll find a prayer that you can read or personalize, leading you into a time of talking with God about what you've learned. Finally, at the end of each lesson, you'll find a takeaway for the day in the margin—a key learning you can meditate on throughout the day. Each daily lesson should take 20-30 minutes.

Whenever we think about a commitment of time such as this, we tend to think about all of the other obligations and responsibilities that are pressing in upon us. So, I want to offer you some incentive. In this Bible study, your investment of time will directly impact how far you get in your battle against worry.

We spend tremendous amounts of time worrying. Time and energy are fuel for worry. So, to fight worry, we need to divert that time and energy into a different place. Every minute you spend on this Bible study will be a minute that you block or battle worry. What's more, you'll discover that God will exponentially multiply the effectiveness of each minute you devote to doing your lessons and use the time you used to spend worrying—time you now can devote to the life-giving thoughts and activities God desires for you.

Although you can do this study individually and reap benefits, it is designed to be done with a group for encouragement, support, and accountability. So, I encourage you to gather once a week with a group of women to watch the weekly video teaching, discuss what you are learning, and pray together. Each video message is designed to follow and compliment the content that you have studied during that week. Whether or not your group watches the video, it's so helpful for you to share your struggles and victories in your battle against worry. As you do, you'll encourage one another and find strength to complete the study and put into practice all that you're learning.

Special Features

God's waiting to give you victory over worry, but you need to get equipped in order to follow His way. So, scattered throughout the study you'll find some special features that will help you implement God's battle plan, including a map of the land of Canaan (page 11) and three extra tools for battling worry. In addition, I have identified many additional Scripture verses on worry and peace that I was unable to include in the study due to space limitations, and I would love to text/e-mail you one beautifully designed Scripture card for each day of your study (seven each week, forty-two in all). These verses are designed to share on social media as well as be used as inspirational desktop or cellphone wallpaper. Go to barbroose.com/scripturecards/.

A Final Word

Though I don't know your name or the specifics of your worry battle, God does. He was thinking of you as I was writing, my friend, and He's got a victory with your name on it. Are you ready to claim that victory over worry in Jesus' name? I hope so!

There's a message that God repeats several times to Joshua in chapter 1, and the full expression of this message is the final word that I want to leave with you: "*Be strong and courageous. Do not be frightened, and do not be dismayed, for the* LORD *your God is with you wherever you go*" (Joshua 1:9 ESV).

May this verse serve as a strong shield for you throughout our study. During the next six weeks, you're likely to battle not only worry but also circumstances that might tempt you to give up on this study. Don't give up, my friend! Winning against worry may be hard work, but you are not on your own. We are in this together, and our mighty, unfailing God is on our side!

Barb

Introduction to the Book of Joshua

When I began studying the Book of Joshua, it was overwhelming trying to take in all of the unique names and places. If you've ever watched a superhero or fantasy movie, it takes a few scenes before you're able to acclimate your mind to an unknown world with new names and places. But once you do, you're fully able to embrace and immerse yourself in the story.

Studying the Book of Joshua has been one of the greatest learning experiences of my life, and it is my prayer that you'll feel the same. To help you on your way, I want to introduce you to some key background information as well as important people and places you'll need to become familiar with in order to get the most from this study.

Background

The Book of Joshua is the sixth book in the Old Testament and the first book in a section of historical books. While the book shares the same name as the Israelites' leader who succeeded Moses, it is a historical narrative of their campaign into the Promised Land. It begins forty years after the Israelites escaped from slavery in Egypt. During those forty years, the Israelites traveled around the wilderness of Egypt's Sinai Peninsula, a low-population desert region that is the only strip of land connecting Africa and Asia. Key events in the wilderness shaped Joshua's future as the Israelites' leader.

One important feature to note about the Book of Joshua is that many of the events are tied to events in the first five books of the Bible (Genesis, Exodus, Leviticus, Numbers, Deuteronomy). Part of your in-depth study experience includes learning how so many biblical details are divinely woven together. Even as you read how humans made mistakes, turned away from God, or even opposed God, you'll be encouraged by how God still brought together hundreds of years of promises and plans for His glory.

Five Key Themes

There are many themes in the Book of Joshua, but for the puroses of our study, we will be focusing on five that relate to winning the worry battle:

1. God is our source of courage and strength in uncertain or undesired circumstances.
2. God fights for us.
3. Failure to follow God leads to pain for us and can create unpleasant consequences for others.
4. God never loses track of His promises to us.
5. God gives us the choice of how we want to live, but we must live with the consequences of our choice.

Four Phases

The Book of Joshua consists of twenty-four chapters that commentarians[1] group into four sections representing the four phases within the book:

1. *Chapters 1–5*: The Israelites arrive on the eastern side of the Jordan and cross into the land. (Arrival)
2. *Chapters 6–12*: The Israelites battle Canaanite kings and inhabitants to take the land. (Acquisition)
3. *Chapters 13–21*: Joshua oversees the division of the land to individual tribes. (Allotment)
4. *Chapters 22–24*: The Israelites receive instructions about serving God in the Promised Land. (Allegiance)

People to Know

There are a few groups of people who are key players in the story we will be studying.

Israelites: Hebrew descendants of Abraham and a people specially favored by God as a result of God's promise to Abraham centuries before.

Twelve Tribes of Israel: The Israelites, who are named after Abraham's grandson Jacob, whom God renamed Israel, are divided into twelve tribes descending from the sons of Jacob (Reuben, Simeon, Levi, Judah, Zebulun, Issachar, Dan, Gad, Asher, Naphtali, Joseph, and Benjamin; see Genesis 49:1-28). However, on his deathbed Jacob adopted Joseph's two sons, Manesseh and Ephraim, as his own so that he could give Joseph's descendants a double blessing (see Genesis 48:5-22). Often lists of the twelve tribes replace Joseph with Manesseh and Ephraim and omit Levi, the priestly tribe that did not receive territory (we will learn more about that in our study):

Reuben	Simeon	Judah	Zebulun
Issachar	Dan	Gad	Asher
Naphtali	Benjamin	Manesseh	Ephraim

Canaanites: These are the people already inhabiting the land of Canaan. There are many different tribes of Canaanites, including the Amorites, Hittites, Hivites, Perrizites, Jebusites, and others.

The Geographic Area

Since the Book of Joshua captures the story of the Israelites' entry into the land of Canaan as well as their campaign to capture the land, it's important to understand the geographic area. Canaan, also known as the Israelites' Promised Land, is the land God promised to give Abraham and his descendants. God first made this promise to Abraham (Genesis 15:18-21) and then confirmed it to Abraham's son Isaac (Genesis 26:3) and finally to Isaac's son Jacob (Genesis 28:13). This land included the territory "from the Red Sea to the Mediterranean Sea, and from the eastern wilderness to the Euphrates River" (Exodus 23:31). Canaan was "the land bridge between Mesopotamia and Egypt and between the Mediterranean and the Red Sea."[2]

As mentioned in the introduction, a map of the land of Canaan is provided on the following page. Each week you'll use the map to match people and events. In my own experience, when I became familiar with certain cities on the map, I could better visualize the sequence of events as I studied them. I want you to have that same benefit.

On the Map

The Land of CANAAN
(The Promised Land)

SCALE OF MILES
0 5 10 15 20 25 30

The Great Sea

ARAM

Sidon

Tyre

Dan (Laish)

Kedesh

Hazor

Lake Huleh

ASHER

NAPHTALI

MANASSEH

Golan

Sea of Galilee

Ashtaroth

Rimnon

ZEBULUN

Dor

Megiddo

ISSACHAR

Ramoth-gilead

MANASSEH

Taanach

Shechem

River Jordan

Joppa

EPHRAIM

Shiloh

GAD

AMMON

DAN

Bethel

Ai

Gezer

Jericho

Gilgal

Shittim

Bezer

BENJAMIN

Ashdod

Jerusalem

Bethlehem

REUBEN

Ashkelon

JUDAH

Dead Sea

Gaza

Lachish

Hebron

River Arnon

Ziklag

MOAB

Beer-sheba

SIMEON

EDOM

ON THE EDGE OF UNCERTAINTY

Facing Our Fears

Joshua 1

MEMORY VERSE

"Have I not commanded you? Be strong and courageous. Do not be frightened, and do not be dismayed, for the Lord your God is with you wherever you go."

(Joshua 1:9 ESV)

On a scale of 1–10, how would you rate your current level of worry? One article reported that the average person spends 55 minutes per day worrying, and that persons struggling with generalized anxiety disorder worry about 310 minutes per day.[1]

For years, I felt like I was buried underneath the oppressive weight of worry. King Solomon's observation in Proverbs 12:25 described my life then so well! He wrote, "Worry weighs a person down; / [but] an encouraging word cheers a person up." I was truly weighed down by worry. Many people live with this reality every day. One woman told me that she has had to manage anxiety all of her life and is now seeing a medical doctor about it because she is having panic attacks in her sleep that are waking her up at night. Most of her worry, she says, is unfounded. She is not alone in that regard. In fact, five hundred years ago Michel de Montaigne said, "My life has been full of terrible misfortunes most of which never happened."[2]

I can relate. One day I stood in my kitchen, swiping at the tears rolling down my face. Was I worried after a difficult phone call or a fight with a friend? No, I was sobbing over a horrible "mental movie" playing in my mind about one of my girls getting into a car accident while driving to her friend's house.

Have you ever cried over a horrible mental movie that you made up in your mind? In my case, the mental imagery seemed so real! I could see the accident scene and myself running and screaming toward a mangled car with hazy smoke rising from the wreckage. In my mind's eye, I could see the EMTs pulling me away from my child as they said, "Ma'am, she's gone. Let her go, ma'am." I could hear my screams and feel my heart pounding as tears streamed down my face. Then, I snapped back to reality.

Do you ever get caught up in a mental movie of a worst case scario? Perhaps right now you're worried about a family member, a friend, or your job situation. Whenever we're not sure what will happen or we're afraid of what might happen, it's easy for us to jump to the worst case scenario and let it play in our minds over and over again. Each time we play that mental movie, we end up worn out and drained.

Maybe mental movies aren't your issue, but you spend your days on pins-and-needles, believing that bad news is around every corner. Most of us have spent time worrying about the bad things that could happen—whether they involve our families, jobs, finances, health, or futures. By definition, the word *worry* means to torment yourself with, or suffer from, disturbing thoughts. This week we will explore the "what if" game we all play and how the first step toward victory over worry is facing our fears and turning our focus to God and His promises. And by the end of the week, you'll have a three-step plan that will help to jump-start you toward your own personal victory!

DAY 1: EIGHT-LEGGED WORRY

I've spent most of my life being afraid of spiders—big ones, little ones, hairy ones, even fake ones that people post on my Facebook page because they think it's funny to share them with me. Haters.

When I was nine years old, I saw a spider in my parents' bathroom while brushing my teeth. I called for one of my parents to come and get it for me. Even now, I remember that it was a little black spider on a wall not bothering anyone at all. My parents told me that I needed to kill it, and they wouldn't let me run away from the challenge. I knew that spider was going to get me, but it never did. It was probably laughing at the scared little girl wearing pop bottle glasses and holding a toothbrush.

Through the years, I've battled the persistent worry that any spider that sees me will try to chase me and bite me. In fact, even a contained spider makes me jittery. Two of my children had the same teacher when they were in second grade, and this teacher kept a tarantula as a classroom pet. Though the furry creature lived in a glass enclosure with a lid on the top, that wasn't enough to keep the lid on my rampant imagination.

What if one of the kids left the lid ajar?

What if the spider pushes the lid off on its own?

What if the spider gets out, crawls into my daughter's backpack, and makes it to my house?

What if my girl volunteers to bring the spider home for the weekend?

And that's only a few of the "what if" worries that were on my list.

Do you have your own "eight-legged worry"? What are you afraid of, and what are the related "what if" worries that you're struggling to deal with?

Write one of your fears inside the spider and some of the related "what if" worries on the legs.

Extra Insight

One report indicates that 38 percent of people worry every day, most often in the early morning or late evening.[3]

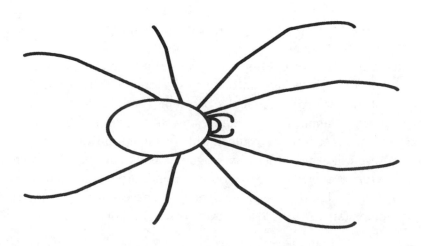

I'm embarrassed to admit that I avoided the girls' classroom for both of those school years. And, of course, nothing that I worried about actually came true!

The origin of the word *worry* is an Old English word meaning "strangle." Have you ever felt that a worry was strangling the life right out of you? Another word for "worry" is "anxiety," which is derived from a word related to a tightening feeling in the chest or throat.[4] Notice how the words themselves indicate that a thought in your mind can create real physical reactions in your body. So, it's not just your mind that worries; your body worries, too.

Circle the physical symptoms that tend to accompany your worries:

Headache	**Short temper**	**Nausea/ fluttery stomach**
Racing heartbeat	**Trembling**	**Inability to concentrate**
Sleep Issues	**Over/Under eating**	**Excessive crying**

I've never met a person who says, "I'm so glad that I'm a worrier. Being a worrier is the best thing that has ever happened to me!" In fact, the question that I'm asked most often is, "How can I stop worrying so much?"

But before we get to that question, I want to ask a different question: How does worrying begin?

Worrying begins when you face unpredictable situations and you don't know what will happen next. I don't like it when I can't see what's coming. I'm not comfortable when I can't name or prevent the dangers that lurk down the street and around the corner. All of those unknown events in my life and yours are what we call uncertainty.

Uncertainty is defined by "what if" questions. Uncertainty invites insecurity. When we are uncertain, our hope is that if we can fill in the answers to the "what if" questions, then we'll feel safe and stable.

Are you dealing with an area of uncertainty in your life? If so, what feels open-ended and unknown?

Over the next six weeks, you're going to learn from the Israelites how God will empower you to win over worry, and you don't have to be a chronic worrier to benefit from our study. There's a Chinese proverb that advises, "Dig the well before you are thirsty."[5] If you don't have many worries, then use this time to dig your well. Uncertainty can find us at anytime, so now is the time to prepare for it.

To prime the pump, let's look at Jesus' words in Matthew 6. This is one of the best known teachings on worry and a great place to begin our study. Jesus'

25 "That is why I tell you not to worry about everyday life—whether you have enough food and drink, or enough clothes to wear. Isn't life more than food, and your body more than clothing? 26 Look at the birds. They don't plant or harvest or store food in barns, for your heavenly Father feeds them. And aren't you far more valuable to him than they are? 27 Can all your worries add a single moment to your life?"

(Matthew 6:25-27)

timeless words are relevant to our lives today and would have encouraged the Israelites during Joshua's time, too, if they could have heard them.

Read Matthew 6:25-27 in the margin. What three things does Jesus tell us not to worry about?

1. _____

2. _____

3. _____

What do His words about the birds tell us about God's desire to take care of us?

Look at verse 27. How productive is worry?

How do Jesus' words apply to your life *right now*?

You don't have to worry because God will take care of you, no matter where you are or what you are going through.

Jesus taught on a hillside to a crowd of people from all walks of life. But everyone in the crowd had something in common: they worried. How do we know they worried? Because Jesus was teaching on it!

If you've been feeling guilty because you worry too much, I encourage you to let go of that guilt. Jesus taught on worry because He knew that it would be a struggle for us. You aren't alone in your struggle.

In the remaining verses of Matthew 6, Jesus continues talking about worry as well as the solution for worry. We'll talk about that solution throughout the weeks of our study. Today I just want to reassure you that you don't have to worry because God will take care of you, no matter where you are or what you are going through.

Now, are you ready for more encouragement?

Apply It: Monday Motivation

Today you may have a long list of items on your to-do list or a lot on your mind. Regardless of your personal schedule, begin working to memorize this week's memory verse. You'll encounter the main message of this verse in many ways throughout our study, but I hope this message will encourage you today.

Look up the verse and fill in the blanks:

"Have I not commanded you? Be _____ and _____. Do not be frightened, and do not be dismayed, for the _____ your _____ is with you _____ you go."

(Joshua 1:9 ESV)

2. Repeat this verse aloud two times, letting it settle into your heart.

3. Rewrite the verse substituting your name for every *you*:

"Have I not commanded _____? Be strong and courageous. Do not be frightened, and do not be dismayed, for the LORD your God is with _____ wherever _____ go[es]."

(Joshua 1:9 ESV)

4. If God is with you wherever you go, how should that change your perspective on the unknowns and uncertainties of your life today?

5. What hope does this verse bring to your life this week?

Prayer

Dear God, I am grateful that I can be strong and courageous with You by my side. There is nothing that I will encounter today on my own, because You are with me. I pray that the words of Joshua 1:9 will sink deep into my heart and mind. Remind me of these words if I begin to worry today. Thank You for being with me wherever I go. In Jesus' name, Amen.

DAY 2: ARE WE THERE YET?

Imagine that you're flying to a foreign country you've never visited before. You have a lot of excitement while you're planning, applying for passports,

and packing bags. Even parking in the long-term parking lot brings a sense of adventure as you head toward the terminal and your destination. Hours later, all of that excitement shifts to uncertainty when you hear the captain announce in multiple languages that the aircraft is making its final descent. When you look out the window while still thousands of feet in the air, everything across your visual landscape seems strange and new. Maybe the homes and highways look different. It's then that you lean over to your traveling companion to start making guesses about what things will be like in this unfamiliar place.

Write below a few things you would wonder or worry about the first time you visited a foreign country:

¹ After the death of Moses the Lord's servant, the Lord spoke to Joshua son of Nun, Moses' assistant. ² "Moses my servant is dead. Therefore, the time has come for you to lead these people, the Israelites, across the Jordan River into the land I am giving them."

(Joshua 1:1-2)

Read Joshua 1:1-2 in the margin. What does God tell Joshua about Moses?

What does God instruct Joshua to do?

As the Book of Joshua opens, millions of Israelite men, women, and children stand clustered together east of the Jordan River. Before his death, their leader Moses had gathered all the people to tell them what to expect, what to do, and how to live. Even with all of that new knowledge, I'm sure there were a few people with some lingering worries or concerns. Now Moses has died, and their new leader, Joshua, stands before the people.

The Israelites have wandered in the desert for forty years, and a new home awaits them just on the other side of the Jordan River. Any journey that takes forty years is sure to be a fascinating story. In fact, the books of Exodus, Numbers, Leviticus, and Deuteronomy convey the lively events of the Israelites' extended sojourn in the wilderness. We are going to dip into a few verses within these books in order to gather some important details that we should know as the Israelites finally arrive at the entrance of their new homeland.

Read Deuteronomy 1:1-5. How many days should it have taken for the Israelites to make their journey to the Promised Land?

After the Israelites fled from Egypt and Pharaoh's army through the Red Sea, they journeyed around and through the wilderness. Early in their journey, Moses received the Ten Commandments from God on Mount Sinai, bringing them down to the people before they reached the edge of Canaan, the Promised Land, for the first time. Yes, the Israelites actually made it to the Promised Land decades before they finally were able to enter it. Unfortunately, they allowed uncontrolled fear and worry to control their actions and ultimately rob them of receiving God's promised blessing at that time.

We read in Numbers 13 and 14 that when they reached Canaan this first time, Moses sent twelve men out with a list of questions to answer as they checked out the land. The men returned after forty days to give their report. Ten spies told scary stories about giants in the land, but Joshua and a man named Caleb told a different story. Joshua countered the fear-inducing report of the other ten spies with a favorable report. In the following verses we see a powerful picture of who Joshua was and what he believed.

Read Numbers 14:6-9. What did Joshua and Caleb beg the people not to do in verse 9?

Now read verse 10. How did the people respond to the plea of these two men?

In the remaining verses of chapter 14, there's a pretty intense scene going down. Moses begs God not to destroy the people for their rebellion, and God doesn't destroy them but instead changes the trajectory of their lives. He does not change the promise but only the time line for receiving what was promised.

Read Numbers 14:29-34 and answer the following questions.

Why was God angry with the Israelites?

Who would die in the wilderness? Who were the two exceptions?

On the Map

The Israelites were gathered in Shittim (shi-teem) by the Jordan River across from the city of Jericho. Locate Shittim and circle it (page 11).

Who would God carry safely into the Promised Land?

Instead of a short journey, how long did God sentence the Israelites to stay in the wilderness?

The Israelites had justified their rebellion because they feared for their children's lives. "Our wives and our little ones will be carried off as plunder!" they had cried (Numbers 14:3). In a sense, they were blaming their fear on their concern for their families. So, it's ironic that God would promise to carry their children safely into Canaan while allowing anyone older than twenty, except for Caleb and Joshua, to die in the wilderness over the next forty years.

I used to blame my problem with worry on certain issues in my life, especially motherhood. For many years, I felt trapped in worry because I was a mom. This meant that I was a pro at answering every "what if" question with a worst-case scenario. Author and journalist Lenore Skenazy calls it "'worst first' thinking."[6] Instead of taking responsibility for my lack of trust in God when it came to my kids' lives, I blamed my worry on the media, rising crime, or any other handy issue that concerned me as a mother looking out for her kids.

What do you blame for your tendency to worry in one or more areas of your life?

"Father, if you are willing, please take this cup of suffering away from me. Yet I want your will to be done, not mine."

(Luke 22:42)

What consequences to your worrying can you identify? In other words, how has worry impacted your faith, health, or relationships?

In Luke 22, Jesus is preparing to be crucified. After celebrating a final Passover with the disciples, He walks to the Mount of Olives overlooking Jerusalem. It's in this moment that Jesus prays to God about what is to come.

Read Luke 22:42 in the margin. Circle the word *if*. Then underline the word *Father*.

Uncertainty beckons us to ask "what if," but Jesus doesn't worry about the *what*. At the point of great stress and fear, He focuses on the *Who*. Jesus knew what was to come and didn't want to go through with it, yet notice His final words: "Yet I want your will to be done, not mine." Jesus was victorious because He kept His focus on God, not His circumstances.

Take a moment for a quick self-inventory.

Why do you want to claim victory over worry?

How will your life be different if you stop worrying?

Why do you think that God wants you to be victorious over worry?

When I contrast Jesus' "Father, if..." to my usual "What if...," I realize that worry weakens when I remember God is with me. It's true for me and it's true for you, too. You can't worry and trust God at the same time. When you say "Father, if...," you acknowledge that even if bad people make bad decisions that hurt or harm you, God is still with you. Likewise, when you say "Father, if..." and then bad situations break your heart or kill your dreams, you've already invited God's power to bring about blessing in the midst of brokenness and pain.

As you enter into the worry battle, cast a broader vision than just wanting to stop worrying so much. Yes, you can be victorious over worry; but that's not the main victory. The greatest victory in triumphing over worry is that you can more clearly and closely see God being active in your life and circumstances. Worry may obscure our vision and our route to the Promised Land God has for us, but God is with us and will show us how to win the battle!

Apply It: Tool Tuesday

When we talk about our worries, we're guaranteed to focus on our worries. So, let's shift our focus away from our worries and end today by immersing ourselves in a hefty dose of God's wisdom. Throughout our study, I will be introducing several tools and techniques inspired by the Book of Joshua that I've used personally with great results. Today I'd like to share a technique that

> **Worry weakens when I remember that God is with me.**

Today's Takeaway

God's wisdom always triumphs over my worry.

will enable you to fight worry with wisdom. God's wisdom is always more effective than your worry, so let's apply His wisdom to your worry battle today.

Wisdom Over Worry

1. In the first blank, write one area of your life that you are worried about today, and in the second blank, write the outcomes that you fear, such as harm, loss, pain, regret, shame/embarrassment, abandonment, disconnection, or even death.

   Today, I am worried about _____

   because I fear _____.

2. Though you can use any Scripture verse in this step, today let's use this week's memory verse, Joshua 1:9, as we practice the technique together. This step rephrases the words of the verse to bring your worry under the authority of God's wisdom, allowing God's wisdom to swallow up your worry.

   God, help me to be strong and courageous as I deal with

   _____.

   (situation or area of your life)

   I will not be frightened of feeling/experiencing

   _____

   (feared negative outcome)

   because I know that You are with me all the way.

   (Based on Joshua 1:9)

3. Use this technique whenever you start thinking about this area of your life. I suggest writing the statement on a sticky note or a note in your phone. The faster you speak God's wisdom over your worry, the sooner God can crush your worry before it begins to make you miserable.

   Reflect: How does it feel to submit your worry to God's wisdom?

Prayer

God, just as the Israelites were afraid of the giants in the land of Canaan, sometimes I am overwhelmed by the giant worries in my life. Yet because You are with me, I don't have to worry or fear. Today I am worried about _____, and I need to give that worry to You. I can't do anything about it, but You can! In Jesus' name, Amen.

DAY 3: JOSHUA

When I was fourteen years old, my parents announced that we were traveling from our home in Ohio to Oklahoma to visit my grandfather and his wife. Not only had I never been to Oklahoma, but I'd also never met my mother's biological father. My grandparents divorced when my mother was young, and she and my grandmother moved across the country. After that, my mother stayed in touch with her father through mail and phone calls but was able to visit in person only a few times. Then years later, this opportunity arose for my parents to take us kids to meet and connect with our grandfather for the first time.

I don't know how many times my eleven-year-old sister, seven-year-old brother, and I asked our parents "Are we there yet?" during the eighteen-hour drive, but I do remember that we were about an hour away from my grandfather's home when my dad whipped the van into a parking lot. My patient father never raised his voice during our cross-country drive, but after listening to three kids bicker and complain across five states in the heat and traffic, he needed a break. Dad jumped out and ordered us out of the vehicle. Then one at a time he lifted each of us, positioning us on top of a different corner of the van. From my corner, I could see my dad stalking off across the hot pavement. Alone.

By the time the Israelites reached the edge of Canaan, I'm pretty sure there were a few parents who felt tired and weary like my dad. They had spent decades packing and unpacking, listening to whining children or spouses, and wondering when their long journey was really coming to an end.

One of the major themes in the Book of Joshua is that God always keeps His promises. Canaan wasn't just an idea that God came up with while the Israelites were wandering around. God wasn't panicked, thinking that maybe He should get them off the road and settled because they'd been adrift for too long. In fact, God was about to bring a promise to pass that He'd made many centuries before. Long before the Israelites arrived at the eastern edge of the Jordan, God had made a promise to a man named Abram, later renamed Abraham.

Read Genesis 12:1-3. What did God promise Abram?

At the time of the promise, Abram didn't even have any kids. In fact, he and his wife, Sarai, later renamed Sarah, were childless, which was devastating to a woman in that society. Yet, since God always keeps His promises, eventually the beloved Abraham and Sarah had a son named Isaac. And one day their son Issac had twin sons named Jacob and Esau. Jacob would become the father of twelve sons, who would become the ancestors of the twelve tribes of Israel. It was the descendants of those sons who were gathered on east of the Jordan with Joshua, standing on the edge of a promise that was finally coming true.

Read Joshua 1:3. What has God promised Joshua?

God repeated to Joshua the same words He spoke to Moses in Deuteronomy 11:24. This promise was very personal to Joshua, for as you learned yesterday, years ago Joshua had toured the beautiful land that God was now about to give to the Israelites. He knew the bounty of the land, but he also knew the uncertainty and dangers that awaited them there, too.

Read Joshua 1:4-5. What are the next promises that God makes to Joshua?

Joshua had been a warrior, and God knew that his military leadership experience would be needed once the Israelites crossed over the Jordan River into Canaan. Though Joshua may have seen the land, he didn't know what it would take to capture the land. All he knew was that God promised to be with him every step of the way and to deliver victory.

This is a good time for us to find out a little more about Joshua. While the book is named after him, it's more of a narrative of the Israelites than it is of their leader. In Scripture we see that he is a powerful and pivotal influence long before the full-length historical book bearing his name begins. In fact, Joshua appears in the books of Exodus, Numbers, and Deuteronomy, allowing us to assemble a composite picture of this man of faith.

Joshua was born in Egypt during the Hebrew captivity. He lived through the plagues, the first Passover, and the great escape from Pharaoh through the Red Sea. We know he was at least twenty years old when the Israelites fled from Egypt because, as we saw yesterday, he and Caleb were exempted from God's curse on the rebellious people following the spies' expedition into the Promised Land (Numbers 14:29-30). Like the other Israelites, Joshua had an eyewitness perspective on seeing God protect and provide for His people, as

well as discipline them. He served in many important roles before God called him to the biggest leadership challenge of his life.

Read the following verses, and draw a line to match each of Joshua's earlier roles with the appropriate Scripture.

Exodus 17:9   **Assistant**

Numbers 13:1-16   **Warrior**

Exodus 24:13   **Spy/Explorer/Scout**

Joshua's name itself gives us some insight into his ultimate role or calling. Interestingly, this name by which he is remembered was not his original name.

Read Numbers 13:8, 16. What was Joshua's original name?

The name *Hoshea* means "salvation" in Hebrew.[7] But later Moses renamed him Joshua, which is translated Yehoshua, or Jehoshua, meaning "the LORD is salvation."[8] Scholars have suggested different reasons for this name change, with some indicating that it was a common practice when appointing a second-in-command (see Genesis 41:44-45 and Daniel 4:8). Perhaps Moses recognized that Joshua would save many. Whatever the reason, there is even deeper meaning to be found here. Like much of the Old Testament, the Book of Joshua contains symbolism that is fully revealed in the New Testament, and one of the most prevalent symbols is Joshua as a type for Jesus. In fact, Jesus' name means Joshua in Hebrew.

Read the following passages of Scripture, noting the parallels between Joshua and Jesus:

Joshua 1:10-11   **Joshua was the _____**
                        of the people.

Hebrews 2:10   **Jesus was the leader (captain/pioneer) to**
                        bring people to _____.

Joshua 1:11   **Joshua will lead the people across the**
                        Jordan to take possession of the

                        _____

                        that God was giving to them.

John 10:10 (KJV)	Jesus says that he came to give us life more
	_____.
Joshua 10:12,13	Joshua commanded the sun to
	_____.
Mark 4:39	Jesus commanded the wind to
	_____.
Joshua 10:24	Joshua told the warriors to put their
	_____
	upon the necks of the defeated kings.
Hebrews 10:12-13	After Jesus' victory on the cross, Jesus'
	enemies are now _____.

Whenever we're not sure about what we're facing, the most important thing that we can do is look up.

Though we can clearly see these parallels from our vantage point, to Moses and the Israelites Joshua was simply a strong leader. And so it was that after forty years in the wilderness, Joshua became Moses's successor around the age of sixty years old. Taking on the leadership of an entire nation was a big deal. However, Joshua had dug his well before he needed it. Not only had he practiced a lifetime of faith, but he also had been mentored and prepared for this role for many years by Moses. While Moses's mission was to lead the Israelites out of captivity and through the wilderness, Joshua had a different mission.

Read Deuteronomy 1:38. What does God tell Moses about Joshua's future?

I'm not sure if Joshua knew in advance that he'd lead the Israelites into the Promised Land. But if he did, I imagine that despite years of preparation, the weight of that impeding role still would have felt heavy on his shoulders.

We're no different. With every new opportunity comes an unknown frontier. So, whenever we're not sure about what we're facing, the most important thing that we can do is look up.

When have you felt the weight of an unknown frontier or new responsibility?

In what ways did you "look up" during that time?

Now, let's move to the final chapters of Deuteronomy where Moses addresses Joshua directly in front of the Israelite people.

Read Deuteronomy 31:7-8. What are the first four words that Moses speaks to Joshua?

What would Joshua's two responsibilities be?

1.

2.

What guarantee does Moses give Joshua regarding God's help?

Now read Deuteronomy 34:9. What happens when Moses places his hands on Joshua?

What's important for us to remember is that the same God who promised to be with Joshua promises His presence to us, too. Whatever you're wondering or worried about today, God is present with you right now. You aren't facing that situation alone.

Read Hebrews 13:6 in the margin. Why do we not need to fear?

So we can say with confidence,

"The LORD is my helper, so I will have no fear. What can mere people do to me?" *(Hebrews 13:6)*

Joshua's early life is a reminder that every role and responsibility we are assigned matters. Moses wouldn't pick just anyone to be his assistant. He must have discerned something special in Joshua before choosing to work closely with him. Each time we read about Joshua in Scripture, he gets the job done. He is a man of deep faith who isn't swayed by his powerful access to Moses, and he doesn't use his military influence for selfish means.

Throughout this study, you'll see Joshua as a leader who isn't perfect but who loves and trusts God—a God who makes bold promises and removes all uncertainty about the future. Essentially God says, "Joshua, I will make sure that whatever you see will be yours," and this promise is a reflection of God's faithfulness and power. You'll also see how Joshua responds by making bold decisions as well as learning from his mistakes.

Joshua knows that the Canaanites aren't going to give up their land without a fight. Likewise, the Israelites have to do more than just announce, "We're here!" They actually have to go into the land and fight for it.

The Bible is filled with promises for those who are God's daughters and sons—those who trust and follow Him. Do you know what God has promised you? More important, have you claimed those promises for yourself? We could spend an entire week or more exploring the verses in Scripture that convey what God says He will do for us, but for now let's just look at a short list

Look up each verse and write a summary of what God has promised. (If you want to read more of God's promises, check out the additional verses in the sidebar.)

Additional Verses: God's Promises

Psalm 27:1, Psalm 34:17, Psalm 86:5, Isaiah 40:29, Jeremiah 29:11, Malachi 3:10, Mark 11:24, John 3:16, John 3:36, John 8:36

SCRIPTURE	WHAT GOD HAS PROMISED
Exodus 14:14	
Philippians 4:19	
Isaiah 41:10	
James 1:5	
1 John 1:9	

As you reflect on this list of promises, which ones are the hardest for you to believe or claim for yourself?

What are some things that get in the way of you believing these promises for you? Circle the ones that might be true for you:

Fear   **Doubt**   **Shame**   **Guilt**   **Pride**

Now pick one of the promises in the chart on page 28. Consider choosing a promise that might be difficult for you to believe at this time. How will you apply that promise to a situation or worry that you are facing today?

God's promises are so precious! At the point when your knowledge of God's promises outweighs the number of your fears, you'll be on your way to victory over worry.

Apply It: Wisdom Wednesday

"Sometimes in our pain or in our panic we forget God, we forget His promises."[9]
–Sheila Walsh

Prayer

Dear God, thank You for being a God who keeps His promises! You have been faithful to Your people throughout all the generations. God, You know the places of uncertainty in my life today; and instead of panicking about them, I choose now to embrace the truth of Your promises. In Jesus' name, Amen.

DAY 4: BE A WARRIOR, NOT A WORRIER

My oldest daughter is an officer in the army and a graduate of the United States Military Academy. She reported to boot camp at West Point less than a month after graduating from high school.

I wish that I could tell you that I was all celebration and smiles before she left for six weeks of arduous training. Frankly, I was a worried wreck. It didn't matter that I knew all of the information about how long training would last and when we could expect phone calls. I still had more questions—questions that the army couldn't answer for me. I had loud, booming questions that demanded to be heard over and over again until I couldn't sleep but only cry.

What if I missed her call?

What if she got hurt?

> A warrior knows who she is and doesn't get swept away by worries that tell her otherwise.

What if she hated the army and wanted to quit?

What if she didn't need me any more?

All of those "what if" questions weighed down my heart and mind. Have you heard of WWJD or What Would Jesus Do? Well, I was suffering from a form of uncertainty called WWHMe or What Would Happen to Me? I wanted the answers to those "what if" questions because I needed to know if I was going to be okay. I wanted answers so that I could predict the likelihood of pain or loss and try to avoid it. However, my WWHMe only resulted in more worry.

While my daughter was heading off to learn how to be a warrior, I was becoming an expert worrier.

Today, we're talking about the difference between a warrior and a worrier. While the words begin and end with the same letters, what happens in-between tells the real story. When I think about the "a" in warrior, I associate it with "anchored." A warrior knows who she is and doesn't get swept away by worries that tell her otherwise. Conversely, I associate the "o" in worrier with "overpowered." A worrier is overpowered by her negative thinking patterns and cannot control them.

You're about to have a front row seat in the "How to be a warrior" class. Your instructor is God, and He's teaching the brave and valiant Joshua about what it means to be a warrior in his heart and mind before he ever steps on the battlefield.

Look up Joshua 1:6, and write it below:

Let's think about the word *be* for a moment. This two-letter word is one of the most important verbs in the English language. The word *be* communicates a state of being or identity. Think about it like this: *be* is the action form of *me*.

In Joshua 1:6 above, circle the word *be* and draw two arrows from that word to the words *strong* and *courageous*.

Because God gives this command to Joshua, we know that God recognizes that as a human, even Joshua's heart and mind might wander toward worry. In the face of uncertainty and danger, worry whispers to each of us.

Put a check mark by the worry whispers that you've encountered recently:

 _____ *What if you can't fix this?*

_____ *What if you fall apart or fail?*

_____ *What if you don't get answers?*

_____ *What if you are unhappy?*

_____ *What if you don't get what you want?*

_____ **Other:**

I love how God seems to be helping Joshua dig an anti-worry well before he needs it.

Read Deuteronomy 31:6, Deuteronomy 31:23, and Joshua 1:7. What two words are repeated in each of these verses?

_____ **and** _____

It seems that God really wants Joshua to pay attention to this command to be strong and courageous. This is interesting since Joshua is a valiant warrior who has bravely faced down opponents and put his life at risk many times in the past on the battlefield. Yet, this time God knows that the task before Joshua isn't only about fighting an enemy, because Joshua's attitude will have an influence on the people around him.

What are some of the things that Joshua might worry about as the leader of the Israelite families and army?

Imagine having leadership over several million people as well as an army that is preparing to go to war against many different enemies. I'm not sure if I would be able to sleep at night because of the thousands of "what if" questions going through my mind. It's here that I feel like maybe Joshua and I have something in common. If God had to continually remind this valiant soldier, faithful assistant to Moses, and spy who stood up to the people, then maybe Joshua might understand what it's like for me to battle worry, too.

If you asked the people who are closest to you whether you are a worrier or a warrior, which do you think they would choose? Why?

Let's revisit some of the verses that talk about having strength and courage. These verses contain a unique addendum explaining what will happen as a result of having strength and courage.

What are some of the outcomes that God promises Joshua will experience if he leads with strength and courage?

Joshua 1:7

Joshua 1:8

Joshua 1:16

God sure likes to repeat Himself! However, God repeats Himself not because He needs to but because He knows that we need it.

If you're Joshua standing on the edge of uncertainty with a new job and daunting new responsibilities, strength and courage may not feel natural or normal. Still, God's command to Joshua to be strong and courageous isn't a command to fake it until he feels it. Joshua is to actually assume strength and courage before he ever goes into his first battle. God wants to dig Joshua's strength-and-courage well and fill it up before he ever needs it.

When it comes to winning your worry battle, God wants to do the same for you. If you give God the time and commitment now to retool your heart and mind, then He will set you up for victory before worry even shows up to start a fight.

Apply It: Temperature Check Thursday

Worry Wheel Exercise

When we talk about winning against worry, our goal isn't perfection but to glorify God by allowing Him to reshape our hearts and minds. Even though there isn't an objective measuring tool to see where you are as you advance toward victory, you can take "temperature checks" to get a general picture of how you are doing.

Here's a baseline temperature check for you to measure the amount of worry in these important areas of your life. This isn't a grading tool for your performance. It's intended to be a "focus moment" between you and God.

On the following page, put a check mark in the category that captures the amount of worry you feel in that area of your life:

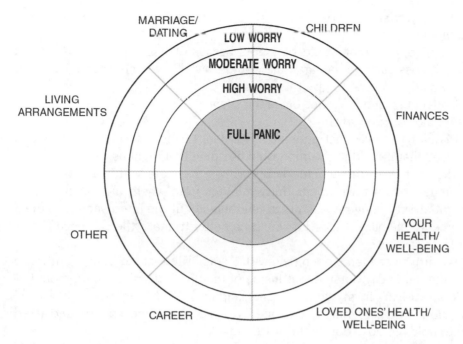

MARRIAGE/
DATING   LOW WORRY   CHILDREN

           MODERATE WORRY

            HIGH WORRY

LIVING
ARRANGEMENTS   FINANCES

            FULL PANIC

                                      YOUR
                                      HEALTH/
                                      WELL-BEING

OTHER

                              LOVED ONES' HEALTH/
CAREER   WELL-BEING

Today's Takeaway

God digs and fills my strength-and-courage well even before I need it.

You'll have a chance at the end of our study to do a follow-up worry wheel exercise to see how you've grown and how God has worked within your heart and mind. For today, make a personal commitment in prayer to move from the mind-set of a worrier to a warrior!

Prayer

Dear God, I want to be a warrior, not a worrier! I'm tired of feeling overpowered by my worries, and I'm ready for You to bring me victory! You've got a greater vision for my life than just to stop worrying, and I want to walk in that greater vision.

God, I want to be strong and courageous like Joshua. I hear Your words to him, and I affirm that the same promise You made to him applies to me today. In Jesus' name, Amen.

DAY 5: YOUR PERSONAL PLAN TO VICTORY

Once upon a time, I jumped out of an airplane because of Joshua. It's true.

As I prepared to give a message about Joshua, the creative team at my church suggested that I find something courageous to do in homage to Joshua's courage. They also wanted to film my courageous act. As the team considered a variety of ideas, a voice in the back piped up:

Extra Insight

"Barb, you should go to the zoo and touch a tarantula. That would be courageous."

I replied, "No, that would be stupid because I'd scream so loud that I'd probably pass out, and the tarantula would crawl all over me. Then I'd die, and there would be no one to give this message."

Undaunted, another voice broke the silence.

"Would you go skydiving?"

I couldn't say yes fast enough. Of course, I called my husband first and promised that I wouldn't die and would be home that night as ususal.

The next day I drove three hours across the state with a producer and videographer to a town about thirty minutes from where my parents live. I thought about calling my parents to tell them about the jump and invite them to come watch, but I decided it would be better to make the call once I knew that I was still alive!

We arrived at a large open field with a small white-sided building. It was a beautiful, quiet day outside, but inside of me the "butterflies" were more like spiders skydiving in my stomach and landing with a thud. My eight-legged worry now had a parachute that I hoped would open in time. I prayed and asked God to hold me close during this wacky adventure.

Next week I'll share the other half of that story. For today, let's see how God prepares Joshua for the challenge that looms in front of him. Whenever God gives us a promise, God also gives us a plan.

Study this Book of Instruction continually. Meditate on it day and night so you will be sure to obey everything written in it. Only then will you prosper and succeed in all you do.

(Joshua 1:8)

Read Joshua 1:8 in the margin. This is the personal plan for victory that God gives Joshua. Identify and write the three steps to this plan below:

1.

2.

3.

What is the end result of this plan?

First, God calls Joshua to study the Law or commandments God gave Moses in Deuteronomy. Next, God calls Joshua to meditate or ruminate on the Law. God knows that the foundation for Joshua's military and leadership decisions depends on what else Joshua is thinking about. Joshua needs to let the words roll around in his heart and mind until they become the fuel for his thoughts, attitudes, and behaviors. It's in that meditation and engraining that Joshua can be obedient, which is the third and final step. The word *obey* appears more than seventy times in Deuteronomy alone and over four hundred times in the Bible. Obedience is the evidence that we love God, and as Psalm 119:2 tells us, the result of our obedience is joy: "Joyful are those who obey his laws / and search for him with all their hearts." God promises that if Joshua follows this personal plan for victory, then he will find success in fulfilling his God-given purpose.

This personal path to victory that God gives Joshua summarizes much of what Moses taught the people in his final speeches before his death, found in Deuteronomy 30–33.

Read Deuteronomy 30:16 in the margin. Compare the words of this verse to Joshua 1:8 on page 34, listing the similarities below:

For I command you this day to love the LORD your God and to keep his commands, decrees, and regulations by walking in his ways. If you do this, you will live and multiply, and the LORD your God will bless you and the land you are about to enter and occupy.

(Deuteronomy 30:16)

While Joshua's purpose was to lead the Israelites into the Promised Land, his priorities were to stay connected to God's teachings, be committed to obedience, and remain conscious of God's activity within and all around him. Having a job that would require life and death situations as well as the leadership of millions, Joshua surely knew that he had to put first things first.

Read Matthew 6:33 in the margin. Where should we look first for answers to life's uncertainties, and what is the promised result?

Seek the Kingdom of God above all else, and live righteously, and he will give you everything you need.

(Matthew 6:33)

What does it mean to seek God first above all else?

If there are worries on your heart and mind today, how does this verse encourage you?

Several years ago a study of Protestant churchgoers in the United States asked participants a lot of questions about church life and personal spiritual disciplines, such as Bible engagement. While 90 percent of the surveyed churchgoers reported that they wanted to live to please Jesus, the percentages were lower related to self-reported Bible engagement:[11]

Percentage	How Often They Read the Bible (Outside of Worship)
19%	every day
25%	a few times a week
14%	once a week
22%	once a month or a few times a month
18%	rarely or never

What are your thoughts in response to this data? Which category best describes your own Bible reading habits?

If you are feeling any shame or guilt over your Bible reading habits or knowledge, kick those feelings to the curb right now! The point of sharing this data and asking these questions is not to make us feel guilty but to help us take an honest look at our Bible reading habits so that we can refocus.

As the staff member responsible for Bible study and small groups at my church for many years, I loved January because that's when people were highly motivated to begin new Bible reading plans, join small groups, or attend church for more consecutive weekends. Our groups and classes would be jam-packed with people highly motivated to stick with their discipleship plan. Yet by Easter the numbers and enthusiasm mellowed. We could always count on a repeat swell in September with a lull before Thanksgiving. After Christmas, people would make the same promises to ring in the new year. This predictable pattern merely highlights our tendency as human beings to need ongoing encouragement to refocus on spiritual habits such as Bible study and prayer.

God's plan for success is simple: read/study God's Word, meditate, and obey. Yet we struggle with following this plan. Why? To put it simply, we allow the urgent to hijack the important.

If Joshua were standing before you, he could list the many responsibilities he had as a military leader. Yet God's plan for Joshua's victory had nothing to do with his military duties or a daily task list. God directed Joshua's attention toward the maintenance of his soul. For all of the obligations and situations in his life screaming DO, God invited Joshua to BE—to focus on God and God's Word, and to live out of that focus. Like Joshua, God calls us to devote time every day to the soul-enriching, life-ordering practice of focusing on Him.

Is your life more about DO or BE right now? What's screaming DO in your life?

> God's plan for success is simple: read/study God's Word, meditate, and obey.

What do you think God might be able to do in your life if you were a little less DO and a little more BE?

While we'll practice meditation a little later in our study, today I want to draw our attention to a rhythm that God asks Joshua to follow regarding meditation. This is an important observation in our preparation for the worry battle.

Different translations of Joshua 1:8 use a variety of adverbs to describe how often Joshua was to study God's "Book of Instruction." We see words such as *continually* (NLT), *always* (NIV), and *shall not depart* (KJV, NRSV, ESV). These words aren't about motivation; rather, these words lean toward discipline and routine.

A routine is a consistent, persistent rhythm. The personal path to victory that God gives Joshua is a consistent, persistent rhythm that will lead us to victory as well.

Why do you think that worry-thoughts often outpace God's wisdom-thoughts in our minds?

What can you do to increase your wisdom-thoughts so that they outnumber your worry-thoughts?

One of the tips that I use to decrease my worry-thoughts and increase my wisdom-thoughts is to write and post Scriptures. I like to write verses on note cards and tape them in my prayer closet or on my desk. Sometimes I write a date or a note about why that verse is important to me. Posting Scripture cards enables me to see verses often and, over time, commit them to memory. I encourage you to give it a try, too.

Some people say that a regular rhythm or routine is a slippery slide into legalism, but there is an important distinction between the two. A routine can be successful if your heart is open and willing. But if you're just doing something to check off the box, then that's where legalism comes in. And here's an important caveat when it comes to reading and studying God's Word. Even if sometimes you don't feel like doing your Bible study but you keep showing up with God's Word because you want His way of life to flourish in you, then that's a good thing! It's all about the motive of your heart.

Today's Takeaway

Whenever God gives me a promise, God gives me a plan.

What are your challenges when it comes to creating a consistent, persistent routine of Bible study? Check all that apply, and circle your greatest challenge.

_____ Family schedule/responsibilities

_____ Work schedule

_____ Lack of Bible knowledge or confidence

_____ No accountability

_____ Unsure about making the commitment

_____ Easily distracted

_____ Not sure what the problem is

_____ No desire

Which of these questions points to a step that might be actionable for you?

_____ Who would be willing to listen to you talk about the challenges you are facing and help you find solutions?

_____ Who might be willing to do a daily or weekly Bible reading or study plan along with you?

_____ How can technology help you (such as an app that limits notifications or facilitates Bible reading/study)?

_____ Would it be helpful to create a special space in your house, such as a corner in a room or a favorite chair, where you can put your Bible study materials and a comfy blanket?

Apply It: Freedom Friday

At the end of each week of our study, you are invited to celebrate any victories that you've experienced during the week. Maybe your victory this week is that you started this Bible study. Or perhaps your victory is that you worried a little less. Did you memorize this week's memory verse? If so, that's a cause for celebration!

What victory are you celebrating this week?

Prayer

Dear God, there's so much that we can learn from reading and meditating on Your Word; and when we put it into practice, we find victory in our lives. Help me to deal with the distractions that keep me from regularly reading and studying the Bible. Give me wisdom and practical solutions so that I can establish a consistent, persistent relationship with You. Amen.

_____ is at the heart of our uncertainty.

Joshua 1:3-5—God's promise to Joshua

1. _____ Victory
   God will enable Joshua to do all that God has called him to do.

2. _____ Victory
   Victory over the fear of not having enough.

3. _____ Victory
   Victory over the human desires that can put a wedge between us and God.

Victory—God is _____ us and _____ us in every circumstance, real or imagined.

Matthew 6:25-27—Jesus' words about worry

Matthew 26:39, 42—Jesus demonstrated "God, if . . ." praying

We can flip our fear to faith when we move from "_____ _____ . . . ?" to "_____, _____ . . . ."

This is my command—be strong and courageous! Do not be afraid or discouraged. For the LORD your God is with you wherever you go."

(Joshua 1:9)

See page 206 for answers.

GOD, KNOCK DOWN MY WORRY WALLS!

Letting God Fight for Us

Joshua 2–6

It's go time! This week in our study the Israelites are preparing to enter Canaan.

The Book of Joshua is the culmination of a series of important events chronicled in the first five books of the Bible. In any journey, we appreciate the destination much more when we understand the steps leading up to it. So, let's quickly recap why God sent the Israelites to Canaan specifically.

Abram left his home in Ur in the land of Mesopotamia (Asia) and traveled toward Canaan with his wife, Sarai; his father, Terah; and his nephew, Lot. But on the way they decided to stop and settle in Haran (Genesis 11). After Terah died, God told Abram to pack up and go on to Canaan, promising that He would make Abram—later renamed Abraham—a great nation. Once he arrived in Canaan, God appeared to Abram at Shechem and promised that one day that land would be given to his descendants (Genesis 12). This is how the term *Promised Land* came to be; it was a land promised to God's people.

Abraham's great-grandson, Joseph, was sold into slavery by his brothers and, after many trials and tribulations, eventually became second in command to Pharaoh and the one who saved all of Egypt as well as his own family from starvation during a famine. After reconciling with his brothers, Joseph relocated his entire clan to Egypt, where they multiplied greatly over the generations (Genesis 37–50). In time a new pharaoh, who feared their number, made the Israelites their slaves (Exodus 1). Many years and generations passed before Moses became the leader of the Israelites and led them out of Egypt toward the Promised Land of Canaan. And as we saw last week, they spent forty years wandering in the wilderness.

When it was finally time to enter the Promised Land, God didn't send the Israelites rushing across the river in boats, shouting, "We're home!" to the inhabitants of the land. God prepared them. He gave Moses instructions to give the Israelites on how to establish a new way of life. They had been slaves for centuries and then desert nomads, so they needed a framework for how to live in a permanent homeland. Then, God prepared Joshua to lead them into the land and fight the inhabitants.

That's what I love about God. Whenever He's planning to do a new thing in your life or mine, He takes the time to prepare us—often before we even realize it. Sometimes God prepares us by allowing us to feel the pressure of discontentment so that we go looking for Him. Perhaps in the past God has prepared you for a new season by allowing some things to be eliminated from your life so that you could spend more time with Him. Or perhaps preparation has come as you have been divinely directed to a church, Bible study, or spiritual friendship. However it may come, preparation always takes times.

When it comes to battling worry, there's no magic pill. Frankly, there's no magic Bible study, either. But what you will find is that God works in phases

and stages. This week you will be invited to allow God to prepare your heart for what He wants to do in order to help you win your worry battle. As we see how God prepares the Israelites for the new life they are about to experience, I hope you will think and pray about how God wants to integrate these themes into your life.

DAY 1: LET GOD LEAD

As part of the preparation for the Israelite's campaign in Canaan, Joshua's first military action is to send two spies to scout out the city of Jericho, which is just west of the Jordan River about eight miles north of the Dead Sea. The morning after the two spies return from scouting in Jericho, Joshua and the Israelites move to the edge of the Jordan River and set up camp again.

Take a moment and put yourself in the place of an Israelite woman who might be your age. Like you, she carries on the functions of everyday life—all while camped across from her new homeland. She prays to God about her worries and sometimes tries in vain to answer those "what if" questions on her own. When she attempts the latter, she struggles with a difficult case of WWHMe (What will happen to me?). She may not have any answers, but she knows that once she crosses the Jordan, nothing will be the same again.

As she stands and looks at the Jordan, she wonders if God will do the same thing He did forty years before to the Red Sea, parting the waters. But unlike that time, she and her family aren't being chased down. Even so, how are they going to get all of their animals, tents, cookware, and clothing across to the other side? What if something goes wrong? What if the stories about that land aren't true?

Wait, now she hears Joshua's leaders giving instructions about how they are to cross the river.

Read Joshua 3:2-3. What instructions are the people given?

Now it's moving day! Our Israelite sister hears the leaders say that the priests are bringing the ark of the covenant, and the people are not to move until the ark passes by.

The ark of the covenant is a physical symbol of the presence of God.[1] It often is carried before the Israelites into battle, and now it will lead the people across the Jordan and into the Promised Land.

The ark is the symbol of certainty that the people need. They don't know all the plans for what will happen next, but they follow the God who does.

If we were to drill down the leaders' instructions to a simple one-liner, it would be this: Let God lead.

Read Joshua 3:4. How far behind the ark are the people supposed to follow?

To provide perspective, a half-mile or two thousand cubits is equivalent to a fifteen-minute walk behind the ark. Such a distance would keep someone from making the fatal mistake of touching the ark, as Uzzah does in 2 Samuel 6:6-7.

For me, the distance is also symbolic. Sometimes we are in a hurry when we are trying to get somewhere or get something done. We pray and ask God for help or favor, and at first we're patient. But when we feel God is taking too long to get us where or what we want, we can be tempted to rush ahead of God.

Has there been a time when you rushed ahead of God instead of waiting on His timing? If so, how did you know that you were rushing ahead of Him?

We know that we're rushing ahead of God when we start to worry about details. On the other hand, when we wait on God to lead us, we are far enough back to let Him pave the way for us.

When I sensed God calling me to leave my full-time job at my church, it took all of my new-found discipline to really let God lead. For years, I had run ahead of God whenever I got excited about something. I'd plot and plan, and then I'd go into action—like the time I bought a house without telling my husband. Yes, you read that right!

Letting God lead my transition into full-time ministry happened in phases. In fact, God began to prepare me over a year before I actually made the transition. I'd had many times of fasting and praying, as well as wise counsel and confirmation from many. Of course, I felt the burden of uncertainty, but I discovered that I had to leave a lot of space for God to go before me.

One of the most important lessons I learned in that experience is that when I do leave God plenty of time and space to go before me, God clears the way for me to see where I should step. Just as the ark was a half-mile ahead of the people so that they could see, without obstruction, God moving before them,

Fast facts about the ark of the covenant (from Exodus 37:1 7):

The ark was made from acacia wood, the same wood found in the area where the Israelites camped.

The ark was a sacred chest measuring 45" x 27" x 27".

The ark was overlaid with pure gold on the inside and out, as well as gold moldings and rings.

Poles were inserted in the rings so that the ark could be moved without anyone touching it.

Moses was instructed to place the stone tables inside the ark.

On the Map

The Jordan River is connected by three bodies of water. Locate these bodies of water on the map (page 11), and trace the lines connecting them:

1) Lake Huleh, the most northern and smallest body of water (70 feet below sea level;

2) the Sea of Galilee (200 feet below sea level); and

3) the Dead Sea, which is where the Jordan River ends (1,290 feet below sea level). This great drop is how the Jordan got its name, which means "Descender."[2]

we've got to take a step back as well. God is at work in our lives, but if we're too busy trying to work our own agenda, we might miss what He's doing.

As I reflect on the people following behind the ark, I'm reminded to do two things:

1. Let God lead.
2. Don't try to overtake His lead.

Which one is more difficult for you: letting God lead or trying not to overtake God's lead? Why?

When we're in the midst of uncertainty, we don't know which way to go. Yet how often have I run ahead of God, trying to find my way in the dark, yelling, "It's okay, God. I've got this!" That usually happens right before I run smack into a wall of worry!

Letting God lead means waiting for God to move. We wait, even as we're sitting in uncertainty. Even as the WWHMe questions bombard our minds, we wait. That's why techniques such as Wisdom Over Worry (page 22) are so helpful. God often makes us wait for Him to move, but He makes us wait so that we can watch Him move miraculously in our favor.

When is it hardest for you to wait on God, and why?

Read Joshua 3:9-13. What will the people realize by the end of the day?

At the beginning of verse 10, Joshua says, "Today you will know that the living God is among you." Even though the Israelites have never been through what they are about to experience, Joshua reminds them that they will experience God's presence in the midst of their uncertainty.

According to verse 13, what will happen to the water as the ark of the covenant leads the people into the Jordan?

At times I have a bad habit of reading something in the Bible and thinking, "Oh, that's nice." If you're familiar with the stories of God parting the Red Sea and the Jordan River, you might be thinking the same thing. But wait.

God parted an entire body of water, friends.

Each time I read about the massive movements of God in Scripture, it reminds me to remember the massive movements of God in my own life. At the end of today's lesson, we're going to do an exercise to capture some of those movements, or moments, in our lives. But for now, let's keep reading.

Read Joshua 3:14-17. How were the banks of the Jordan River at this time of year?

What happened once the feet of the priests touched the river's edge?

As soon as the priests' feet touch the edge of the overflowing river, the water withdraws. Commentarians debate the actual population of Israelites crossing the Jordan; however, a number believe that there are an estimated two million Israelites at the time of the crossing.[3] Add in a bunch of sheep, goats, tents, carts, and a few cranky toddlers, and you can easily imagine the sheer magnitude of the crossing.

As I think about our imagined Israelite girlfriend crossing the river with her family, I wonder what she is thinking as her feet walk across dry land that previously was covered with deep water. I'd like to think that if I was in her place, I would be amazed and would promise myself never to forget that moment.

After all of the Israelites cross the Jordan, God instructs Joshua to do something to make sure no one ever forgets what has happened.

Read Joshua 4:2-4 and answer the following questions:

What does God instruct Joshua to do?

Once the men are chosen, what task are they to carry out?

Letting God lead means waiting for God to move.

Extra Insight

The Book of Joshua records the establishment of seven stone memorials throughout the Israelite campaign in the Promised Land.

Now that the Israelites have crossed over the Jordan, they establish a new campground at Gilgal. As you can imagine, the talk in camp is about what the people have just experienced. Think about the dinnertime discussion that our Israelite sister might have with her family as they reflect on the incredible miracle and movement of God. Picture all the kids asking dozens of questions about how the water drew up and did not drown them.

Rather than let the Jordan-crossing fade into memory, God wants to mark the moment of this epic experience.

Read Joshua 4:6-8. What does Joshua say about the purpose of the memorial?

God commands them to make the memorial so that as they travel by it, they will be reminded of what God did that day. And it won't just be the Israelites who will be reminded; anyone traveling by the memorial might inquire about the stones later and hear the story.

Then Joshua does something that might seem a little confusing.

Read Joshua 4:9. What does Joshua do next?

It seems that Joshua has set up a second set of twelve stones where the priests stood in the Jordan, and the last part of verse 9 indicates that the stones remained in that spot.

Now read Joshua 4:15-18. What happens as soon as the ark of the covenant and the priests come out of the water?

The water may have reclaimed its former place, but the memory of what happened could never be erased. While commentators and theologians have discussed the significance of Joshua's second pile of stones and whether that, too, was a memorial, we know that God ordered at least one memorial that day.[4] And we will see throughout the Book of Joshua that other memorials would be established later.

Just like the Israelites, we need reminders, too. Unfortunately, we're pretty forgetful. I don't know about you, but it's embarrassing how many times I've questioned God's power or faithfulness in my life. Yet when I stop and remember what God has done, that remembering recalibrates my faith.

Just as the Israelites pulled twelve stones out of the water to represent God's faithfulness to each of the twelve tribes of Israel, let's close today by remembering twelve times in our lives when God showed up and blessed us or made a difference in our lives. Because worry is a negative perspective of the future, we must come at worry with the firm facts of God's faithfulness in the past!

Today's Takeaway

Remembering God's faithfulness encourages me to overcome my fears.

Apply It: Monday Motivation

Whenever you're struggling with worry or simply in a bad mood, remembering God's faithfulness can be a powerful and effective way to swing your anxious or grumpy outlook to a grateful attitude.

In the spaces below, write twelve times when God showed up in your life. Here are some questions to assist your memory:

- **Did God answer a prayer about a direction or relationship in your life?**
- **Did you experience a personal encounter with God?**
- **Has there been a divine appointment that changed your life or outlook on life?**
- **Was there a sudden change in your health (or that of a loved one) that lead to an increased connection with God?**
- **Did God provide financially in a way that could be explained only by His intervention?**

1.

2.

3.

4.

5.

6.

7.

8.

9.

10.

11.

12.

Prayer

Dear God, today I am reminded that just as You are the God who pushed back the Jordan, You are capable of making a way for me through the deep and difficult places in my life. Prompt my heart to remember even more times when Your faithfulness impacted my life. In Jesus' name, Amen.

DAY 2: PREPARING OUR HEARTS FOR BATTLE

Extra Insight

Covenant:
An agreement between two people or two groups that involves promises from each side to the other. The Hebrew word for *covenant* means "betweenness."[5]

Word travels fast.

After the Israelites cross the Jordan, word spreads to the Amorite kings west of the Jordan as well as the other Canaanite kings. Those kings aren't going to give up their land without a fight, but they are clearly shaken by the reports they've heard of the God of the Israelites.

Still, Joshua isn't going to rush the Israelites into battle even if the pagan kings are in a weakened state. Instead, he follows God's commands for preparing the people for what is to come. The time has come to re-introduce a ritual and a remembrance.

Read Joshua 5:4-8. Why aren't there any circumcised men in the Israelite camp?

Circumcision was the sign of covenant between God and Abraham. In Genesis, God promised the then-childless Abraham that He would bless his descendants and make them His special people. In return, Abraham would remain faithful to God. The sign or symbol of that covenant was circumcision. It was after Abraham's circumcision that his barren wife, Sarah, became pregnant.

For generations, Hebrew males were circumcised as part of the covenant with God. But the sojourn in the wilderness brought that covenant activity to a halt. Since anyone born in the wilderness was not circumcised and the previous generation had died off in the wilderness as a result of the rebellion, Joshua had an entire generation who had not joined in the sign of the covenant.

While a discussion of physical circumcision can feel a little awkward, the Bible also talks about an even more personal, more important type of circumcision that applies to our spiritual condition. In both the Old and New testaments, God calls His people to beware of an uncircumcised heart.

Read Leviticus 26:40-42 in the margin. What does an uncircumcised heart represent?

These verses tell us that an uncircumcised heart represents unfaithfulness to God, or sin. One commentarian uses the words "wicked" and "hard" to describe an uncircumcised heart.[6] But notice how God extends Himself toward His people with the offer of forgiveness if they will turn back toward Him.

Read Jeremiah 6:10 in the margin. What other body part can suffer from uncircumcision?

Can you think of a time when you were stubborn or closed off toward something that God was calling you to do? If so, briefly describe it.

One of the quickest clues that points to a stubborn heart is the unwillingness to pray. Other clues include avoiding meeting with other Christians or reading our Bibles. And I just want to put this out there: It's possible to sit in church every week or attend Bible study and still have a stubborn heart. I know this from experience!

When we're stubborn or closed off from a relationship, it might seem that we are getting our way, but what's really happening is that we're missing out on the blessing of connection. A covenant is for the blessing and benefit of both parties who have entered into agreement. Marriage is a sacred covenant between a husband and wife. Yet, when one or both are stubborn or closed off, the relationship suffers. If the behavior continues, the relationship is at risk of dying.

In the New Testament, the debate over how to view circumcision created a lot of bad feelings between Jewish and Gentile believers. Even though both groups accepted Jesus Christ through faith, there was a segment of Jewish believers, called Judaizers, who wanted Gentile believers to be circumcised before being accepted into the Christian community.

This debate created division in the church, and the apostle Paul had to step in to provide insight and direction.

40 "But if they will confess their sins and the sins of their ancestors—their unfaithfulness and their hostility toward me, 41 which made me hostile toward them so that I sent them into the land of their enemies—then when their uncircumcised hearts are humbled and they pay for their sin, 42 I will remember my covenant with Jacob and my covenant with Isaac and my covenant with Abraham, and I will remember the land."
(Leviticus 26:40-42 NIV)

To whom shall I speak and give warning,
*   that they may hear?*
Behold, their ears are uncircumcised,
*   they cannot listen;*
behold, the word of the
Lord is to them an object of scorn;
*   they take no pleasure in it.*
(Jeremiah 6:10 ESV)

Read the following verses, and then mark the statements below T (true) or F (false):

When you came to Christ, you were "circumcised," but not by a physical procedure. Christ performed a spiritual circumcision—the cutting away of your sinful nature.

(Colossians 2:11)

No, a true Jew is one whose heart is right with God. And true circumcision is not merely obeying the letter of the law; rather, it is a change of heart produced by the Spirit. And a person with a changed heart seeks praise from God, not from people.

(Romans 2:29)

For when we place our faith in Christ Jesus, there is no benefit in being circumcised or being uncircumcised. What is important is faith expressing itself in love.

(Galatians 5:6)

___ 1. A change of heart is true circumcision.

___ 2. If we follow Christ, spiritual circumcision is a requirement.

___ 3. Spiritual circumcision is the cutting away of our sinful nature.

___ 4. If you follow Christ, it doesn't matter if you are physically circumcised or uncircumcised.

We all need a circumcision of the heart.

All of these statements are true. We all need a circumcision of the heart. We all need to give God permission to come in and remove the sinful blockages that cause us to be stubborn or closed off to Him and others.

If you're at the doctor's office and she says, "We need to talk about your heart," you know that whatever she has to say next is serious. We don't mess around with our hearts. If someone needs heart surgery, strict attention is given to finding the best doctor who knows just where to cut and extract or repair the damage.

God is the best heart doctor ever! He knows exactly what's wrong with our hearts, and when we are willing, He performs surgery on us. Just as a doctor uses scalpels and sponges to do her work, the Bible and the Holy Spirit are God's tools.

The key to allowing God to circumcise our hearts can be captured in a word: *willingness.*

What are some of the ways that a willing heart connects with God?

I'd love to hear your responses. Here are a few of my own. A willing heart is eager to worship. A willing heart loves Jesus and His imperfect people. A willing heart trusts God at His word.

Not only does God command Joshua to reinstitute circumcision; another observance is reintroduced in the Promised Land as well.

Read Joshua 5:10-12. What started again in the Promised Land, and what disappeared?

Passover is the final meal that the Israelites prepared in Egypt before God freed them from slavery. It is a symbolic meal to help them remember how the angel of God passed over the homes of the Israelites whose doorposts were marked with the blood of a lamb but brought death to the homes of their enemies. Each element of the meal symbolizes a facet of the Israelites' relationship with God, as well as different aspects of their difficult time in Egypt. Passover also would tie the new generation to the old generation as they remembered how God showed up and moved in their favor in a magnificent way.

Imagine the solemn awe around the fire as the Israelites prepare and celebrate the Passover meal after crossing the Jordan. It would be the first time that this group has experienced this remembrance. Imagine how the mothers and fathers would share snippets of stories overheard from grandparents. The last time the meal had been shared was right before God parted the first deep waters at the Red Sea.

God not only reinstitutes Passover but also brings to an end another aspect of their lifestyle in preparation for their new life in the Promised Land. The next morning they wake up to prepare breakfast, and the manna that God has provided each day in the wilderness is not there.

I wonder if the people panicked—and how long it would take them to remember that they now have the food of the land to enjoy every day. As with them, crisis often calls us to dig deeper in our faith. However, when the crisis has passed, it can be easy for us to settle back into a lifestyle that isn't as hungry for God. It's helpful for us to keep reminders of God's faithfulness close by so that we never forget His goodness toward us.

Extra Insight

Symbolism of Items in the Passover Meal:

Pascal lamb—
Sacrificial substitute for sin.

Bitter herbs—
Symbolizes bitter years of slavery.

Fruit pulp—
Texture like mortar.

Matzo bread—
Represents the hurry of the Israelites to leave Egypt.[7]

Today's Takeaway

My willing heart invites God to battle worry in my life.

Apply It: Tool Tuesday

Count to 12

During yesterday's study, you learned that God instructed Joshua to have the people build a twelve-stone memorial on the river bank, and he also set up twelve stones in the midst of the Jordan. And you ended the day by listing twelve movements of God in your life. Today you are going to refine your list to make your own twelve-stone memorial.

When you were upset as a kid, did your mom or another adult ever tell you to count to ten? That never really worked for me. Counting to ten wasn't enough time for my brain to calm down!

Even as an adult, when I'm facing uncertainty or downright scary times, counting to ten isn't nearly enough to keep me from worrying. What I need in that moment is to re-count specific situations when God has shown up in my life as a way to help me remember to wait for Him to show up in my current situation.

Here's how you can do the "Count to 12" technique:

Step 1: Transfer your list of twelve from page 47 to the stones below by writing just one or two words in each stone.

Step 2: Begin memorizing the list of your twelve memories of God's faithfulness in your life.

Step 3: Turn that list into a prayer you can use when you're in the midst of uncertainty or feeling yourself getting worried over your situation.

Here's a portion of what my prayer looks like:

Dear God, I'm worried about (situation), but I remember all of the times when You've shown up in my life. God, I remember the time when I was in college and my financial aid ran short. Thank You for the woman who made the anonymous $200 donation so that I could stay in school. God, I also remember the time when I was stressed out over my job, and I went away to the retreat center. Thank You for those two days that I spent with You praying. I'll never forget how You opened the door for me to go back to work full-time when so many people were getting laid off at work . . .

Now, it's your turn. Write out your prayer below:

If this exercise resonates with you, consider making your own stone memorial. Look for or purchase some flat stones, and write a word or verse on each one to signify how God showed up in your life. (You can search "stones of remembrance" on Pinterest for some great ideas.) Whether or not you choose to create a literal memorial, keep memorizing your twelve stone memories so that you can quickly recall them in the future to fight worry with God's faithfulness.

Prayer

Dear God, today I need to let You lead the way. You know that _____ is on my mind. Yet, I know that You are the God who will fight for me. So, before I begin thinking about _____ today, I need to focus my heart on You. Show me where I'm not willing to let You lead my life—where I've been stubborn in my sin. I want to have a healthy heart before You. Amen.

DAY 3: FAITH IN UNCERTAIN PLACES

Today we're going to talk about one of my favorite women in the Bible. She's proof that you can face uncertainty with faith over fear or worry. What I love most about her story is that she isn't a picture of someone who says and does all of the right things. She's actually far from that! As we study her background and her life, I hope that you discover that you don't have to be a "perfect" Christian to win your battle against worry or any other struggle that you might be facing today.

Her name is Rahab. She lives within the walls of the city of Jericho, which is located in the Jordan Valley west of the Jordan River. It will be the first military theater where the Israelites will stage an attack.

Jericho's location in the fertile Jordan Valley makes it a primary target for Joshua and his army. Not only is it known as the City of Palm Trees; but its hot, tropical weather produces desirable crops such as date palms, bananas, and a variety of trees.[8]

Jericho has something else noteworthy: a giant wall. The city is built atop a "tell" or mound with a stone wall around its base. Then, there is a retaining wall, like what you might use around your patio or garden, that is twelve to fifteen feet high and about six feet thick. There is a second wall atop the retaining wall that is another twenty to twenty-six feet high. It would be impossible for the Israelite army to enter Jericho through this massive wall.[9]

Giant walls remind me of worry. Whenever there is a worry in my life, it's like a wall that I can't see around, climb over, or tear down.

Are there any worry walls in your life today? If so, identify them below:

Let's get back to the literal walls of Jericho and make our way inside the city to meet Rahab.

Turn to Joshua 2 and put a placeholder here. Read verse 1. What is Rahab's occupation?

There are some who argue that Rahab's description as a prostitute or harlot does not actually mean she was a woman who sold herself to men. There are a variety of reasons people might debate whether Rahab was actually a prostitute. One is the fact that, as we discover in the New Testament, she belonged to the lineage of Christ (Matthew 1:5), and some might not think that a prostitute belongs in such a prestigious family tree. Another reason could be a desire for political correctness. For too many years, women involved in sex work have been judged by Christians, so there are those who might not want the Bible to reflect a judgmental attitude by listing Rahab's profession.[10] However, others point out the likelihood that Rahab was a prostitute not by choice but because of the debt of her family. In fact, "poverty was by far the most common cause of prostitution in the ancient world, as it is in our world as well."[11]

Such a perspective helps us view Rahab's situation and motives through a different lens.

Read Joshua 2:2-4. How does Rahab respond when the king asks her to turn over the two spies?

God uses ordinary, imperfect, and often unlikely people—even the poorest or lowest of society—to accomplish His purposes. Rahab is an example. Yes, she lies to the king by saying that she did not know where the spies were from. But if we focus too narrowly on this behavior, we miss the bigger picture of how God is using her.

One commentator addresses Rahab's actions in protecting the spies this way: "Nonetheless, Rahab acted with integrity based on the limited understanding she had of the God of the Bible at the time. There is evidence here of a changed heart and a changed life. A former prostitute who was once a child of Canaan has become a daughter of Zion."[12]

After the king confronts Rahab, we find out why she protected the spies as well as what she believes.

Read Joshua 2:8-9. What are the first words that Rahab proclaims to the spies?

Here is where we see Rahab demonstrate 100 percent faith at a time when she should be overwhelmed with worry. She begins with the words, "I know…" The Hebrew word for "know" is *yada*.[13] This kind of knowledge is based in conviction, not familiarity.

Just in case you missed it, let's recap: An impoverished prostitute who lives within the walls of a pagan city has made a prophetic statement even in the midst of uncertainty about her life and the lives of those she loves. How brave is that!

Now read verse 10. What are some of the conquests that Rahab has heard about the Israelites? What two Amorite kings did they destroy?

Extra Insight

King Og was the last of the giant Rephaites. His iron bed was thirteen feet long and six feet wide—and was actually put on display. (See Deuteronomy 3:11.)

Just because Jericho has a wall doesn't mean that the people don't hear news from the outside.

Can you imagine the people of Jericho sitting around their dinner tables or whispering to each other, "Did you hear . . . ?" Even though the people of Jericho didn't have newspapers, social media, or a dedicated news channel, word of the Israelites' mighty God penetrated their giant wall.

Did you notice how Rahab attributes all of the victories to God? She doesn't explain away the parting of the Red Sea with science, and she doesn't try to downplay the Israelites' victory over the Amorite kings Sihon and Og. She also notes the change in the attitude of the people in her city.

Read verse 11. How does Rahab describe what happened to the hearts of the people of Jericho?

As a result of their heart condition, what have they lost?

There is an interesting contrast set up here between the Israelites, whom God has instructed to be strong and courageous, and the people of Jericho, whose hearts are melting in fear. Both groups of people are dealing with uncertainty. The Israelites know that they are to go in and take the land, but they don't know what lies in front of them. The people of Jericho are within the walls of their city, but they aren't sure if those walls will be enough to protect them from a God who can part the waters and defeat giants.

When we're facing uncertainty, the story that we tell ourselves about what will happen to us determines whether we will be strong and courageous or allow our hearts to melt in fear.

How is your heart right now? Do you feel strong and courageous, or is there a situation causing your heart to melt in fear? Describe the reason for your response.

He gives strength to the weary, And to him who lacks might He increases power.

(Isaiah 40:29 NASB)

Read Isaiah 40:29 in the margin.

What does God give us when we're overcome with our situation?

My biggest mistake with worry is thinking that if I think or talk long enough, then I can worry my way to peace. It's not true!

Worrying never leads to peace. Worrying only leads to war with ourselves. When we worry, we think that the solution is up to us; and when we can't execute the right solution, we get mad at ourselves.

Write the second half of Joshua 2:11 in the space below:

The people of Canaan worshiped many gods, so it's significant for Rahab to declare the Israelites' God as the Supreme Being—the supreme God in the heavens above and the earth below. It's crazy that a prostitute living inside the walls of a pagan city displays greater faith in God's promises than God's chosen people who have seen God help them overcome their enemies and provide manna to eat each day.

Read Hebrews 11:1. What is the definition of faith?

Faith makes a friend of uncertainty because faith knows that God sits in uncertainty and calls us to walk with Him in the midst of it.

Does thinking of uncertainty as a friend to faith change your perspective in any way? If so, how?

Rahab never saw God split the Red Sea. She wasn't on the battlefield to witness the defeat of mighty kings. Yet she had confidence in God without seeing.

Read Joshua 2:12. What does Rahab ask the spies to do?

Rahab knows there isn't anything that she can do to save her life or the lives of her family. She could choose to throw herself on her bed and cry her eyes out, but instead she steps out in faith and makes a bold request of the spies. Instead of filling her mind with words of worry, she uses her words to ask for a huge, life-changing favor.

Have you ever been that bold?

> **Worrying never leads to peace . . . only to war with ourselves.**

I would like to be that bold more often. God has made so many promises to us, including reminding us that we can be strong and courageous because He is with us wherever we go. But too often I've filled my mind with words of worry instead of using my words to make an ask of God.

Read Hebrews 4:16 in the margin. Circle how we should approach God:

Fearfully	**Arrogantly**
Boldly	**Panic-striken**
Shyly	**Reluctantly**

When we approach God in this way with prayers that only He can answer, how does He respond to us?

Extra Insight

Hebrews 4 reveals that the Promised Land is a symbol of earthly rest, but as we'll see later in the Israelites' story in Joshua, it wasn't designed to be a permanent place of rest.

As believers, our reason for boldness is that our God is the supreme God of the heavens and the earth. If we believe that God is supreme, then that means that He is capable of helping us when we need it most.

Is there a big request that you need to make but have been afraid to bring before God? If so, come boldly before God now, writing your prayer below:

The two spies agree to Rahab's request, but with three conditions.

Read Joshua 2:17-20 to discover the three conditions, and put a check mark beside each one:

___ 1. Rahab must hang a scarlet rope out the window of her home.

___ 2. Rahab must use the rope to climb down during the battle.

___ 3. Rahab's family must stay in the home when the Israelites invade.

___ 4. Rahab can give similar ropes to other people for their homes.

___ 5. Rahab cannot betray the spies.

Rahab knew that she couldn't save herself or her family, but she could follow instructions that would allow her family to live.

Answers: 1, 3, and 5

The same applies to us. We cannot control outcomes. The only thing we can control is how we will handle ourselves or respond during uncertainty. Rahab shows us that faith or confidence in God's supreme power is the only source of real, lasting hope in uncertainty. When we're not sure what's going to happen or how things will turn out, we're to go directly to God and boldly ask for mercy and help. He won't turn us away!

Apply It: Wisdom Wednesday

> *You will keep in perfect peace*
> *all who trust in you,*
> *all whose thoughts are fixed on you!*
>
> (Isaiah 26:3)

Extra Tool

"Jesus, I'm Hanging On to You" 21-Day Challenge

When my mind is racing, sometimes I can forget to pray. So, when I'm in the midst of a high-stress situation, I find it helpful to have a physical reminder to pray.

This technique is simple. For twenty-one days, wear any bracelet and hold on to it whenever you find yourself worrying. In that moment, remember Rahab's faith and affirm God as supreme in the heavens above and the earth below. Then, make your bold ask of God, letting Him know that you'll hold on to Him by faith in the midst of uncertainty.

Check out Barbroose.com/21days to sign up for the 21-day challenge. You'll receive a different Bible verse and prayer via e-mail each day, helping you to intentionally turn toward Jesus in all situations. When you sign up, you also can download a free, beautiful prayer card with powerful Scriptures and reminders on it.

Prayer

Dear God, give me the courage, like Rahab, to pray bold prayers. I know that You are the supreme God of the heavens above and the earth below, and I have nothing to fear. Thank You for always being by my side. Amen.

DAY 4: LETTING GOD FIGHT FOR YOU

Yesterday we heard the first part of Rahab's story, which we will finish tomorrow. She has so much more to teach us about what it means to have

Faith or confidence in God's supreme power is the only source of real, lasting hope in uncertainty.

Today's Takeaway

Worry wages war within, but faith in God's supreme power brings confidence and peace in the midst of uncertainty.

Extra Insight

faith in uncertain places. But today we're going to catch up with Joshua as he is preparing for his first military conquest in Jericho. He has already proved that he is a man of great faith in God—fully aware that God can and will deliver the Promised Land into the hands of the Israelites just as He promised. However, God sets up a dramatic encounter to show Joshua in visual form that He is planning to fight for His people.

Read Joshua 5:13-14. What question does Joshua ask the man with the drawn sword?

What is the man's response?

Joshua sees a man who looks like a threat and asks him a commonsense question: "Are you for us or for our enemies?" (Joshua 5:13 NIV). What's interesting is that Joshua goes over to the unknown man who is holding a drawn sword. Even as a veteran warrior, this is quite a bold thing for Joshua to do.

The man's response might seem confusing: "Neither, . . . but as commander of the army of the LORD I have now come" (Joshua 5:14 NIV).

Does this mean that God isn't on Joshua's side? If so, then all of God's promises made in the first chapter of Joshua are no longer valid.

But, God is on Joshua's side!

Read Joshua 5:15. Why does the man command Joshua to take off his shoes?

The man wants Joshua to know that they are standing on ground set aside by God for a special purpose. The meaning of *holy* is "set apart." It is not Joshua's battlefield that they are standing on. It is God's place of battle. God has already told the Israelites many times that He is going to give them the land, and so the battle is God's to fight.

Joshua may be a valiant warrior and leader, but it isn't his battle. It is God's battle. And the "commander of the LORD's army" has come to remind Joshua of this important fact before he goes into battle.

The same goes for us. Whatever battle you are fighting right now isn't actually your battle.

- You may think that your marriage is for you to save.
- You may think that you're the one who is supposed to get your kid back on track.
- You may think that you're supposed to work three jobs, seven days a week, to save your financial situation.
- You may think that the conflict with your coworker is yours to fix.

Perhaps you're worn out from running around and fighting God's battle that He's waiting to win for you. When the Israelites fled the Egyptians, Joshua was on the run, too. He would have been in the crowd as they looked toward the Red Sea and felt trapped by the water on one side and the deadly warriors bearing down on them on the other. You might say that the people were flipping out!

Read Exodus 14:13-14, and fill in the blank:

God will _____ for us.

What are we instructed to do?

What additional insights do you find in Psalm 37:7; Psalm 46:10; Mark 4:39; and Jeremiah 32:17?

When God fights, He doesn't actually need our help. The worst thing that we can do in the midst of uncertainty is think we're on God's side while expecting God to fight our way. We must beware of filling uncertainty with our expectations.

Are there any fights where you need to back off and let God fight for you?

Read Joshua 6:1-5, 10. What battle plan does God give Joshua, and how will Jericho's wall fall down?

Can you picture this scene in your mind? Remember, there are several million Israelites, including tens of thousands of soldiers. But God tells them to march around the city once a day for six days. Then, on the seventh day, they are to march seven times around the city.

The battle plan is a paradox. Instead of breaking down the wall and fighting, God calls the people to march around the wall and blow some horns. Not only that, but Joshua reminds the people of one important element of their participation.

Reread Joshua 6:10, and summarize the instructions below:

I used to play basketball, and we often engaged in what was called "trash talking." That's when players on each team try to psych each other out, make fun of each other, or make demeaning statements in order to throw off their opponents' concentration. It can be hard to pay attention to the game when there's trash talking going on!

A similar thing happens in the game of life. When we're busy talking, often we're not listening or looking for what God might be doing in us and around us. God is laying the path for our victory, and sometimes we need to stop talking so we don't talk ourselves out of that victory.

What worries do you need to stop talking about because the constant chatter is making your worry worse?

During one stage in life, I talked about my worries to anyone and everyone who would listen. As soon as someone would say, "How are you?" that was license for me to share my dictionary of worry words with them. I thought that I was working through my worry by talking about it, but all of those conversations where I'd rehearse everything I was worried about were actually wearing me out!

Even though I have a community of well-meaning, Jesus-loving friends, I have realized that I need to be thoughtful about how often I discuss my worries. More and more I am realizing that I can short-circuit worry if first I practice being quiet before God and then being patient as I wait. It's okay to share my

struggles with a friend, but only after I have surrendered those struggles to God first.

Do you sometimes struggle to be silent? Are there any triggers such as marriage issues, friendship drama, or parenting issues that make your tongue hard to control? If so, list them below:

Did you know that you can actually discipline yourself toward spiritual silence? I did not think that was possible until I tried it when I realized my worry words were wounding everything and everyone around me.

Richard Foster, author of the classic *Celebration of Discipline*, says that silence is not just the absence of speech but also the presence of active listening.[15] Therefore, the discipline of silence is learning how to see and hear. Once we add this discipline into our lives, we'll learn when to speak and when to refrain from speaking.

I know that many of us are in pressing stages of life with little ones, teenagers, travel schedules, carpools, or aging parents, but it's still possible to practice this discipline. What does it look like practically? Practicing silence is keeping our eyes and ears open toward God while keeping our words to ourselves out of a desire to develop discipline.

Foster offers three suggestions for practicing solitude and silence. Here's a summary:

1.   We can employ "little solitudes" throughout our day, such as using our morning coffee ritual, our morning commute, moments waiting in line at the store, or time after dinner instead of scrolling social media. We intentionally suspend our planning, effort, anxiety, and impatience.
2.   Develop a quiet place in your home. Find a special chair, room, or corner of your patio. When you settle into that spot, practice silence for as long as you are there, whether one minute or one hour.
3.   Withdraw a few times a year for silent retreats for three to four hours at a time.[16]

Do you need to discipline yourself toward more silence? Which of these suggestions might you consider?

> It's okay to share my struggles with a friend, but only after I have surrendered those struggles to God first.

Remember Rahab? She told the spies that the people's hearts had melted in fear, but I wonder how her faith is holding up as the Israelites are marching around the city.

Sometimes I feel like Rahab when I'm not sure what's happening on the other side of "the wall." I know that God is doing something, but I can't see it. Rahab and the people of Jericho must have heard the trumpets blasting and the footsteps of the army marching. For those six days, the air within the city walls would be filled with uncertainty, and each night the army would go back to its camp. But on the seventh day, everything would change.

Read Joshua 6:15-20. How many times do the Israelites march around the wall?

What happens after they shout?

How often do we tell God how we'd like Him to answer our prayers? As we learn from Joshua's encounter with the "commander of the Lord's army," we may think that God is fighting on our side, but actually the battle belongs to God; and He is the one winning the battle. We're invited to participate in the battle, but the winning belongs to God. We experience the win when we're aligned with Him.

Letting God lead means that we wait for Him to move—even when we feel the pressure of uncertainty or the pressure from people who want us to come up with answers that we don't like. The answers will come because God will reveal them to us. God often has us wait for Him to move, but He does it so that we can watch Him move miraculously in our favor and grow in faith.

Extra Tool

Seven Minutes of Silence

The next time you feel compelled to pick up the phone to call someone and complain or express your worries, put your phone in the nearest drawer or purse and practice seven minutes of silence. This would be a great time to silently practice the "Wisdom over Worry" exercise (page 22). Once you accomplish seven minutes of silence, slowly work your way up to a half hour or hour of purposeful silence.

Apply It: Temperature Check Thursday

Today it's time for your weekly check to think about the progress you're making. You've learned a lot of verses as well as a few tools and techniques to use when the worry starts to wear you out. How's it going? Take a moment to honestly assess where you are in your worry battle.

Circle the number that indicates where you are today:

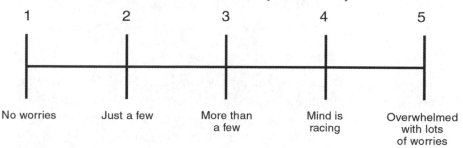

1	2	3	4	5
No worries	Just a few	More than a few	Mind is racing	Overwhelmed with lots of worries

If you circled a 1 or 2, what are you doing to keep worry on a low level?

If you circled 3, 4, or 5, take a few moments and think about the following:

Are you dealing with a new surge of worry, such as from an unexpected situation?

How do you feel about your level of worry? Where would you like it to be by the end of the study?

Which tool or technique can you try for the next five days to equip you to fight back against worry?

Today's Takeaway

We're invited to participate in the battle, but the winning belongs to God.

Prayer

God, it's so hard to wait on You. Often our words are a way of making us feel like we're doing something when we really should be waiting in anticipation for You to move. Thank You for fighting today's battle for me. I will be calm and wait for You to move. Amen.

DAY 5: JESUS, I'M HANGING ON TO YOU!

Last week I told you a little about my skydiving adventure, but I didn't finish the story. As you can imagine, my stomach flip-flopped a number of times while awaiting my turn to jump. During our two-hour wait, I participated in a safety class, learned how parachutes work, and tried on my jumpsuit. I giggled when I realized that I would wear an actual jumpsuit.

But the most important moment of the day happened when my instructor explained the closed metal loop attached to the back of my suit. He showed me the hook on the front of his suit and explained that we'd be tethered for a tandem jump from the plane. I wanted to shout "Hallelujah!" because I had wondered how I would learn how to land safely on my own in such a short time. My jump instructor had more than five thousand jumps on the books at the time, and I felt really good about being tightly tethered to him. I questioned my ability to survive on my own; but as long as I held on to my jump instructor, I knew that I would be okay.

Earlier this week, we peeked behind the wall of Jericho to learn about Rahab, who was given a scarlet cord or rope by the departing spies to use as a signal when they returned. It turns out that Rahab also learned the importance of having something to hold on to!

After following God's instructions and witnessing the wall of Jericho collapse, the Israelites went in to take the city.

Read Joshua 6:22. What did Joshua command the spies to do?

This may seem like an insignificant part of the story, but I so appreciate Joshua's integrity. In the midst of battle, Joshua keeps his word and rescues a woman who doesn't have much value in her society. Not only that, but the Israelites willingly give shelter to her family as well, even though they are foreigners (and likely not believers in the God of the Israelites).

The two spies make their way through the rubble and bodies toward Rahab. Picture the scene of large rocks and debris, dust from the collapse, screams from the people of Jericho, and the sounds of battle.

Review Joshua 2:18. Where are the spies looking to find the rope?

A w_____

Put on your thinking cap for a moment. If Rahab's home was built into the city wall, that cord or rope had to be tied to something that would hold as the walls shook and fell, because we know that the spies were able to find Rahab and her family after the walls crumbled. Some scholars suggest it was the same rope that the spies used to escape; others discount that possibility, noting that two different Hebrew words are used and that displaying the means of the spies' escape would violate what Rahab had pledged not to do. In either case, this scarlet rope in the window served as a reminder each day to Rahab and her family that salvation was coming. They had no idea when or what their rescue would look like, but they could see the symbol of their salvation each day.

Even as they heard the Israelites marching around the city day after day . . .

Even as Rahab and her family heard the frightened cries of their neighbors in the streets . . .

Even as the walls began to shake, crumble, and tumble to the ground, Rahab saw the source of her salvation there in front of her.

There are "scarlet cords" for us throughout the Scriptures—reminders that point us to God's saving power.

Read the following verses. What reassurance(s) do you receive from each?

Psalm 71:2

Psalm 107:19

Isaiah 41:10

Isaiah 59:1

1 Corinthians 10:13

Hebrews 13:6

Once the spies find Rahab and her family, they remove them from the city to a safe place near where the Israelites are camping. Talk about a crazy change in scenery. When we trust God, an adventure always awaits!

So often we think that stepping out in faith is about taking an act of faith, but God has called us to a life of faith. This means that there often will be places in our lives where we don't know what's next. But as Rahab discovered, as long as we dwell with God, He is our safe place.

Now that they have been rescued, what testimony do you think that Rahab and her family are sharing with the rest of the Israelites? And how do you think that her faith encourages them as they move into the Promised Land?

Extra Insight

More verses about God as our refuge: Psalm 18:2; Psalm 71:3; Psalm 91:2; and Proverbs 18:10.

Read Psalm 46:1-3 below:

¹God is our refuge and strength,
*   always ready to help in times of trouble.*
²So we will not fear when earthquakes come
*   and the mountains crumble into the sea.*
³Let the oceans roar and foam.
*   Let the mountains tremble as the waters surge!*

How do these verses describe God?

Once my daughter and I were driving through a heavy thunderstorm on a country road during a tornado warning. In the distance, we noticed low clouds begin to swirl on the ground. I made a quick 180-degree turn in my car and sped in the opposite direction until we found a building where we could wait out the storm. There was nothing like the security of finding safety in something bigger than ourselves! (Later we found out that those swirling clouds were actually a gustnado, not a tornado.)

If you were walking, running, or biking in the midst of a storm, what would finding a refuge mean to you?

Just as Psalm 46 tells us, God is our refuge when we're facing uncontrollable circumstances. He's our place of safety and shelter. Even as our circumstances rumble and roar, God wants to shield us and hold us in His peace and calm. I know that's possible because I've experienced it personally!

Though not all scholars are in agreement, some relate this psalm to King Hezekiah's prayer in 2 Kings 19:15-19 after Sennacherib, the Assyrian king, attacked Judah.[18] This invasion happened about five hundred years after the Israelites entered the Promised Land. King Hezekiah prayed before God, acknowledging the desperation of their situation. In fact, hundreds of thousands of Assyrian troops were right outside of Jerusalem at the time. Not only did King Hezekiah petition God for help, he also appealed to God's character, saying, ". . . then all the kingdoms of the earth will know that you alone, O LORD, are God" (2 Kings 19:19).

Now read 2 Kings 19:35. What happened in the Assyrian camp after King Hezekiah prayed?

Just as God brought down the walls of Jericho, God defended His people by eliminating 185,000 enemy soldiers in one night. Here's the application for us today. We may be facing uncontrollable circumstances, but God's ability to deliver victory is based not on the situation but only on who He is!

I don't know what you are facing today, but the same God who dropped the walls of Jericho is on the job in your life today. You may feel like Rahab waiting to be saved from a difficult situation. If that is you, then hang on to Jesus today!

Apply It: Freedom Friday

Where have you experienced victory in your worry battle this week? Use the space below to record times when you know God was working in your heart and mind to push back worry:

Prayer

God, I'm holding on to You today. In those places where I don't know what will happen, I will keep my eyes focused on Your promise of salvation and hope. Thank You for being my refuge and for protecting me from being mercilessly beat up by the storms of life. Thank You for Your grace, peace, and mercy. In Jesus' name, Amen.

The same God who dropped the walls of Jericho is on the job in your life today.

Today's Takeaway

My victory is determined by who God is, not what I'm facing!

This week we focused on the theme of letting God fight for us as we saw the Israelites cross the Jordan and win the battle of Jericho. Because many of us are so familiar with the story of Jericho, today we're going to bridge that story and the Israelite's next battle at Ai, which we will study in the coming week, by looking ahead to the story of Achan, found in Joshua 7. This story will help us to see that God not only fights for us but He also helps us up when we fall.

Joshua 7:4-5—The Israelites' courage melts away

A meltdown at times can be the very best thing that ever happens to us because it helps us to see the _____.

Joshua 7:6-9—Joshua's meltdown

When we struggle, especially after a meltdown, the most important thing that we can do is realize that we can _____ to _____.

Joshua 7:10—The Lord's response: "Get up!"

The thing that we've got to remember about God is that He _____ our limitations.

Romans 8:1—No condemnation for those who belong to Christ

Romans 2:4—God's kindness and patience

Matthew 14:27—"Take courage. I am here!"

In our worst moments, God reminds us that His promise to give us victory—His promise to be there with us— _____ _____.

Joshua 7:20-21—Achan's confession

God's very best gifts are the gifts that He _____ to me.

Joshua 8:1—God's promise to Joshua about Ai

Sometimes when we see ourselves after falling apart, we can struggle to feel like we
_____ anything good.

Philippians 4:6

Don't _____ about anything; _____ about

everything.

Philippians 4:7

Then you will experience God's _____.

Philippians 4:8

_____ your hearts and minds (thoughts and attitudes) on what

_____ _____.

See page 206 for answers.

WEEK

3

FIGHTING FRIENDS
TO HELP US

Getting into Position

Joshua 7–8

MEMORY VERSE

Study this Book of Instruction continually. Meditate on it day and night so you will be sure to obey everything written in it. Only then will you prosper and succeed in all you do.

(Joshua 1:8)

Once upon a time, there were human remote controls. If you're too young to remember such a thing, just ask anyone over the age of forty! Back then televisions had big, clunky knobs or dials that we turned to change the channel. On any given night Mom or Dad would walk over and turn on the television, settle into a favorite recliner or couch, and then call for the human remote control—otherwise known as one of us kids!

I was often the chosen human remote control. If Dad didn't like the show, he'd say, "Barbara, change the channel." I'd hop up (because I was younger and had good knees) and manually flip the knob. After each channel change, I would stand there and wait for Dad to decide if he wanted to watch that station or move on. Thankfully, there were only four stations back then!

Though I'm no longer a human remote control, there are times in my life when it feels like I'm standing there waiting to change the channel but can't because the knob has fallen off; and so I'm stuck on the worry channel. Or imagine there's a glitch with the cable and all you have access to is WorryFlix, where there's an endless catalogue of movies and shows starring your greatest fears and worries. Some have prequels, sequels, and everything in between; and every full-length feature or episode is filled with painful scenes, crushing emotions, and devastating endings. Yet once you begin watching WorryFlix, it's hard to change the channel. Even as you're brought to tears, you just keep watching those horrible mental images over and over again. Have you ever been kept up at night because you couldn't turn WorryFlix off? Me, too! So, how do we change the channel?

This week we're going to meet some "Fighting Friends" that God has given us for the worry battle. These Fighting Friends will help us get into position to do what I like to call "fighting in faith," which is more about how you fight than who or what you are fighting. These Fighting Friends know how to "change the channel" by disconnecting our minds from WorryFlix. But they don't stop there, because it's not enough to just disconnect and stop worrying. These Fighting Friends actually position us to receive God's power so that we can live the abundant life Jesus promised us. Yes, we want to win the worry battle, but our ultimate goal is to flourish in our faith, not just win over worry.

As we meet these Fighting Friends, we'll see how the Israelites used their own fighting friends to battle back after a defeat and subsequent spiritual meltdown. We should be able to see the worst of our worry struggle through their experience, but we'll also be encouraged as we witness their commitment and faith. So let's get going and get into position!

On the Map

Locate the city of Ai on the map (page 11). (*Hint:* It's slightly southeast of the city of Bethel.)

DAY 1: FIGHTING IN FEAR

As we begin this week, the Israelites are fresh off a major victory at Jericho. The final verse of Joshua 6 tells us that God is with Joshua and that Joshua's fame spreads throughout the land. In social media terms, Joshua's deeds are going viral all over Canaan! Even kings who would never "friend" Joshua are creeping on his page, so to speak, to read the amazing accolades posted by others. Just as God promised, Joshua is meeting with success every place he sets his foot. But even as the celebrations are underway and Joshua is planning for the next battle, there is someone in the Israelite camp who ignored Joshua's directive and sinned while in Jericho.

Today we're going to see what happens after the Israelites suffer a setback and find themselves fighting in fear rather than in faith. Then we'll journey with them as God walks them through the process of re-learning how to fight in faith. Let's set the stage by looking back to the scene before the fall of Jericho. Before the Israelites circle the wall for the seventh time and Joshua gives the order to shout, he instructs them about what they are to do next.

Read Joshua 6:18. What would happen to the entire Israelite camp if anyone took anything dedicated to destruction?

Now read Joshua 7:1. Who sinned and provoked God's anger against all of Israel? What did he do?

In the Old Testament there are times when God allows His people to take spoils and other times when He expressly says "no." In fact, in those instances God uses a special phrase to describe what should not be taken. "Dedicated to destruction" (or devoted things) is the phrase that describes a person, place, or thing that God condemns.

Why do you think God sometimes prohibits the Israelites from taking the spoils of battle, including at Jericho?

Throughout the Bible, God tells us to stay away from anything that will draw our hearts away from Him. The Israelites are a forgetful people. Their time in the wilderness documents this fact again and again. So in order to protect their hearts as they are preparing to enter the Promised Land, God wants His people to acknowledge Him for this wealth of land that He has set before them.

Read Joshua 7:2-5. What do the spies tell Joshua when they return from scouting Ai?

Imagine we're standing among the leaders and soldiers when the spies return. We might see a relaxed posture and smile as one spy says, "We've got this, boss, especially after what we did at Jericho. The boys are tired, so we can leave most everyone at home to rest up for the next battle." In fact, the spies tell Joshua that only two thousand or three thousand men are needed to overcome the Ai army. This is just a tiny percentage of the overall number of Israelite fighting men. But their answer gives us some insight into their heart condition, which can be summed up in one word: *pride*.

Did you notice how the conversation about battle strategy is strictly between Joshua and the spies? In the past, we've seen a pattern of God giving instructions before significant movements are made. But in this case after the Israelites' recent victory, God's input is absent from the conversation.

Why do you think we tend to rely less on God when life is good?

Read Joshua 7:4-5. What happened to the Israelites when they went to fight at Ai, and what happened to the Israelites' courage?

The phrase "melted in fear" might sound familiar, because it's the same phrase that was used to describe the people of Jericho before the battle (Joshua 2:9) and the enemy kings' hearts after hearing about the Israelites' God drying up the waters of the Jordan until the people crossed (Joshua 5:1). Just as their enemies' hearts melted in fear, now the Israelites are experiencing the same horrible sensation. And as we'll see, even their leader, Joshua, melts in fear. In fact, you might say that he has a meltdown.

A meltdown is an uncontrolled expression of hopelessness that happens when we've run out of mental and emotional resources to deal with uncertainty and worry. The key word here is *uncontrolled*.

Recall a time when you had a meltdown. What happened?

Did your meltdown include hysterical crying, hand-wringing, incoherent words, or random movements such as jumping up and down or collapsing to the ground? If so, then we're identical twins when it comes to meltdowns. Other kinds of meltdowns can include social media rants, irresponsible language or behavior, or even a complete emotional shutdown requiring medical care. When we have a meltdown, it's a wake-up call that we need God's help ASAP!

One summer our minivan needed to visit the repair shop. Again. We'd already poured over a thousand dollars into the van in just a few months, and the shop wanted hundreds more for a minor engine repair. Two weeks later the van stopped working again, and this time the shop called with devastating news: a cracked engine block. What happened next isn't difficult for you to visualize: Imagine a tall, black woman wearing a ponytail, pop-bottle glasses, and awful capris. Now imagine her dropping onto her kitchen floor wailing.

While I don't remember how long I lay on the floor wailing, I do remember what was going through my mind: hopelessness. We're never going to get out of this! We're doomed . . .

Did you notice that God was missing from my meltdown? Whenever we face uncertainty without the presence of God, the mounting stress of uncertainty will eventually lead to a meltdown.

What do you think keeps us from inviting God into our uncertainty before we begin the worrying that leads to a meltdown?

You might have said control or self-sufficiency or something along those lines, but it all boils down to pride. I've heard it said that the word PRIDE stands for "**P**lease **R**emember **I D**o **E**verything." It's so easy for us to believe that everything depends on us. When our hearts melt in fear, a meltdown is confirmation that we believe we're all alone in our circumstance. A meltdown means that we cannot move forward—that nothing can be built upon us—in that moment. A meltdown isn't a permanent condition, but it's definitely a painful one for as long as it lasts. Let's take a look at Joshua's meltdown and how he turns it around.

Read Joshua 7:6-9, and write T (true) or F (false) beside each statement:

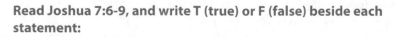

___ 1. Joshua went before the people and pretended that nothing was wrong.

___ 2. Joshua tore his clothes as a symbol of despair and grief.

___ 3. He talked with his officers to figure out what went wrong.

___ 4. Joshua went directly to God with his worry, grief, and sadness.

___ 5. The leaders (elders) stayed with their families and left Joshua to suffer alone.

Joshua turned around his meltdown by turning toward God in his distress. Not only did he express his truest emotions, but he did so without worrying about how others would react. Then he brought his questions to God. Finally, he reminded God of the promises that God had made to His people. Through it all, Joshua maintained an honest dialogue that kept him connected to God. That's how Joshua turned his meltdown around.

Whenever we mess up, the most important action we can take is to go to God and pour our hearts out to Him. At times, we may beat ourselves up for our mistakes or our lack of faith, but God never does!

Apply It: Monday Motivation

Write this reminder on a note card or sticky note and put it somewhere you will see it throughout the day:

I can turn around any meltdown by turning toward God.

Prayer

Dear God, I am grateful for Joshua's example when life goes in the wrong direction. Help me remember to call out to You when I feel a meltdown coming on. You are my help and hope in all situations. Amen.

DAY 2: WHEN "ME" MESSES UP "WE"

Have you ever heard the phrase "flies in the ointment"? It is an expression that explains how small impurities can contaminate the entire batch of a precious product. This common saying has its roots in Ecclesiastes 10:1: "As dead flies cause even a bottle of perfume to stink, / so a little foolishness spoils great wisdom and honor."

Answers: 1. F 2. T 3. F 4. T 5. F

Today's Takeaway

When stress and fear are mounting, I can avoid a meltdown by pouring out my heart to God.

There are several bottles of perfume on my dresser. If I ever see a fly in one of those perfume bottles, I will immediately toss the bottle into the trash! Just removing the fly isn't going to convince me to keep that perfume. One little fly is enough to ruin the entire bottle.

This gross and graphic word picture explains why the Israelites faltered at Ai. One person's sin stunk up the entire Israelite community, affecting everyone. You could say that someone's focus on "me" messed up "we."

Read Joshua 7:13. God tells the Israelites that they will not experience victory until they do what?

Even as the Israelites are in full-meltdown mode, God tells Joshua to get up. It's such a wonderful visual of God shaking Joshua out of his meltdown. God sends a sharp message to Joshua that God hasn't abandoned His promise to the Israelites.

I love how God likes to get situations out into the open so that they can be dealt with. Sin likes to hide in the shadows, but the glory of God always exposes sin in order to heal us.

Some translations use the word *consecrate* in verse 13, while others use *sanctify* or *purify*. The Hebrew word for consecrate is *qadash*, meaning "to be set apart as sacred" or "holy."[1] Whenever God commands the people to consecrate themselves, it is in anticipation of a great move of His power or Spirit among the people.

Look up the following Scriptures and write why God calls the people to consecrate themselves.

Exodus 19:9-11 _____

Joshua 3:5 _____

Extra Insight

"Consecration is going all in and all out for the All in All."[2]

—Mark Batterson

God calls His people to consecrate or sanctify themselves in preparation for Him to move in their presence. Since God is about to move in their presence, they need time to inspect or cleanse their hearts, bodies, and minds. It's not hard to imagine a few nervous Israelites wondering if their secret sinful thoughts or deeds are about to be revealed. Perhaps they wonder if they can't hurry and clean up or cover up any concealed or ignored sin.

Read Joshua 7:15. What is God's judgment on the guilty party?

Not only the guilty party will be destroyed but also all that he has, including everything in his household.

In verses 16-18, we read that in a process of elimination first by tribe and then by clan and family, God reveals to Joshua the perpetrator of the Israelites' sin. Then, Joshua calls Achan forth and asks him what he has done.

Read Joshua 7:19-21. What did Achan take from the spoils of the battle at Jericho?

Extra Insight

"Achan's theft was more than just taking a few coins. The value of the silver and gold represented what an average worker would make in a lifetime."[3]

Achan's first words are, "Truly, I have sinned against the Lord, the God of Israel" (Joshua 7:20 NASB). As he details his theft, Achan reveals that he coveted the items for himself and took them.

I wonder when and why Achan hatched his plan to steal the devoted things. Was he worried that he wouldn't be able to provide for his family in the new land? Did he want to buy some security by having some spoils? Achan's sin whispers to us about two driving human desires: comfort and greed. Add them together and the result is always bad.

We live in one of the wealthiest nations in the world, and yet we worry that we won't have enough. God's generosity pours into our lives every second of the day, yet sometimes we don't feel like we are experiencing God's generosity.

Read Joshua 7:19-21 again. Pay attention to three "I" statements Achan makes in verse 21, and write them in the following blanks:

I _____

I _____

I _____

First, he saw. Then he coveted or wanted. Next, he took. And after he took, he hid the forbidden devoted things. Achan's sin wasn't that he saw, it was that he wanted something that God didn't want for him and then took it.

Maybe you haven't stolen something, but how often do you worry that God won't give you what you want or need?

What if God wants something different for my singleness?
What if God wants something different for my career?
What if God wants something different for my health?
What if God wants something different for my marriage?
What if God wants something different for my fertility?

What if God wants something different for my children?
What if God wants something different for my _____?

Which "what if" question hits home for you? Write it below:

What are you afraid that God won't do for you?

Have you ever made a bad decision in fear because you were trying to secure or protect a good thing? If so, describe it briefly:

It's easy to look down on Achan for his sin. But I've shared the motives of his heart. So have you. How many of us have seen things that we've wanted and "taken" them even though they weren't God's best for us? Even if we didn't steal the items, we bought or pursued what we couldn't afford, what we didn't need, or what ended up distracting us from God.

Read 1 Timothy 6:6-10. According to these verses, what two things should make us content?

> **If we remember God's generosity in those moments when we experience uncertainty, then we can wait in faith for God to act.**

In her Bible study, *Numbers: Learning Contentment in a Culture of More*, Melissa Spoelstra makes this observation in response to 1 Timothy 6:6-10: "Great wealth is just around the corner for those who practice godliness with contentment. The riches may or may not be monetary, but their value exceeds anything that Rockerfeller could have imagined."[4]

Throughout the pages of Scripture, God shows us His generous nature, and we find that He has a track record of generosity toward us:

- He gave us His only Son. (John 3:16)
- He redeems us from death and gives us love and tender mercies. (Psalm 103:4)
- He showers us with the riches of His grace. (Ephesians 1:7-8)

If we remember God's generosity in those moments when we experience uncertainty, then we can wait in faith for God to act instead of making bad decisions because we're worried about protecting a good thing.

Since Achan didn't do this, the consequences of his sin are devastating for him and the entire nation of Israel as they are defeated at Ai.

Read Joshua 7:22-26. What happened to Achan and his family?

How do you feel about this?

If this was difficult for you to read, it's understandable. You may wonder why God, if He is loving, would inflict such a harsh judgment. Perhaps you question other troublesome passages in the Old Testament, wondering if God is somehow different in the Old and New testaments. In his book *When Did God Become a Christian*?, author and pastor David Kalas explores this common struggle, showing that God's holiness and love are both clearly on display throughout the Scriptures, even in difficult passages. Drawing on the writings of Theodoret, a fifth-century monk and bishop from Syria, Kalas points out that sometimes we must look for the truth of God's heart—His desire to love and protect us—hidden within in a Bible story or passage. He writes,

> Theodoret makes a logical connection between God's threats and God's love: "The reason that the God of all threatens punishment, you see, is not to inflict it on those he threatens but to strike them with fear and lead them to repentance, and by ridding them of their wicked behavior extend to them salvation. After all, if he wanted to punish, he would not threaten punishment; instead, by threatnening he makes clear that he longs to save and not to punish."[6]

We see throughout the Scriptures that God wants to save His people from sin—something He ultimately accomplishes through the death of His own Son. Yet as Melissa Spoelstra points out in her study on the Book of Numbers, there are some distinctions in the way that God interacts with His people in the Old and New testaments, who were living under two different covenants. She offers these helpful insights:

> We see differences in the people, circumstances, and methods of interaction between God and His creation [in the Old and New testaments]. What we do not see...are any differences in the character of God. Throughout the Scriptures, God Himself is unchanging....God is both just and gracious in His interactions with His people living under each covenant....One commentator put it this way, "Defiant sin is the

"We must guard against greed so that we can find true riches."[5]
—Melissa Spoelstra

spiritual equivalent of jumping off the Golden Gate Bridge. If biblical warnings sound harsh, they are to prevent that from happening." Like a loving parent who sets boundaries and rules, our loving God wants what is best for us. God wants to protect us, and He knows all too well that sin is never safe.[7]

After reading these observations, what are your thoughts on God's judgment in this story?

Here are a few additional observations to consider as we reflect specifically on Achan's family:

1. The Bible doesn't say whether Achan's family was involved in his theft or in hiding his theft. But the number of items that he took would have been difficult to hide in the ground without someone in the family knowing about it.
2. We know that Achan's family was brought into the valley of Achor, but some commentators question whether they were stoned and burned along with Achan's belongings.[8]
3. There are some verses in the Old Testament that say that God does not punish children for their parents' sin (Ezekiel 18:20) or destroy the righteous with the wicked (Genesis 18:16-33). Yet other verses such as Exodus 34:6-7 say that God will allow the consequences of a parent's sin to affect multiple generations. Regardless of whether Achan's family was innocent or guilty or whether they were stoned and burned, the undeniable truth is that sin has consequences, and often those consequences can bring harm to others.

The punishment for Achan's sin was harsh, and it's okay to struggle with that. But let us consider this: what if Achan, who clearly acted in disobedience even though he knew in advance the penalty for his sin, had not been punished? Achan's influence as a family leader combined with his lack of trust in God and disobedience would have sown seeds of unfaithfulness into his children and grandchildren, affecting their families for years and perhaps generations to come. In this pivotal time for the Israelites as they were entering the land and facing formidable foes, they needed to remain strong in their commitment to obeying God.

In light of all that we have read and studied today, what are your thoughts about Achan's story?

Let's bring this a little closer to home. Has your own life been negatively affected by another family member's sin? Perhaps you grew up in a home where your parents or grandparents demonstrated neglectful or sinful behavior such as abuse, alcoholism, or fear, causing hardship, tragedy, or even death in your family. These negative habits or sins can create strongholds within families. However, family strongholds do not have to hold you hostage. The good news is that through Jesus Christ, you can find freedom from any stronghold, whatever it is!

If you're reading this and are harboring some secret sin, confess it today. God is giving you a space of grace right here and right now. According to Jesus' own words in John 3:17-18 (see the margin), you are not condemned because of the mistakes of your past or even the sins of your family. Jesus came to set you free, if you trust in Him!

As a Christ-follower, I've learned that just as I cannot comprehend God's holiness and the extent to which God hates sin, so I cannot comprehend the depth of God's love and grace. Though it's tough reading stories like Achan's, we should always measure them against the consistent thread of God's character woven throughout the Scriptures and most clearly expressed through His Son, Jesus.

What have you learned today?

Answer as truthfully as you can: Am I holding on to some secret sin/ worry in my life that I need to confess before it is uncovered and/or messes up not only my life but also the lives of others?

Apply It: Tool Tuesday

Search My Heart

Many times there is a spiritual reason behind our worry battle. There may be a seed or root from a past struggle—some misbelief that grows into worry under the right conditions. As long as we don't identify it, we'll be prone to worry.

[17] *"God sent his Son into the world not to judge the world, but to save the world through him.* [18] *There is no judgment against anyone who believes in him. But anyone who does not believe in him has already been judged for not believing in God's one and only Son."*
(John 3:17-18)

Extra Insight

Some Reflections on Achan

1. Our thoughts and feelings are powerful catalysts driving our behavior.

2. Sin is dangerous and can destroy our lives.

3. One believer's sin impacts others, even if it's concealed.

4. God hates sins and gives us commands to protect us from it.

Today's Takeaway

Valuing "me" above "we" often leads to worry and sin; and even undercover worry/sin can create big consequences.

Our daily lives are affected by worldly influences, evil forces, and our own sin. These three areas leave a residue on our hearts, minds, and souls that we can become blind to if we do not allow God to show us the dirt and then ask God to forgive and cleanse us. Use the following exercise to invite God to search your heart:

Step 1: Begin by praying these verses aloud or in your heart:

²³Search me, O God, and know my heart;
test me and know my anxious thoughts.
²⁴Point out anything in me that offends you,
and lead me along the path of everlasting life.
(Psalm 139:23-24)

Step 2: Read each sentence again slowly, focusing on the words. Write below the word or words that stand out to you:

Step 3: Invite God into the process by asking the following questions, writing what you hear in the space provided below.

- **God, what are the roots of worry that I haven't dealt with in my life?**
- **God, reveal to me any habits (whether sinful or not) that block me from wanting to be totally open and close to you.**
- **God, reveal to me any new practices or habits that I need to add to or refresh in my life.**

Impressions during prayer:

As you reflect on your prayer experience, don't allow self-examination to turn into self-condemnation or self-criticism. When we come to God and ask Him to reveal anything that keeps us from close fellowship with Him, we can be assured that it is the conviction of the Holy Spirit working in us and drawing us closer to God.

If you are sensing or hearing whispers such as, "God can never forgive that" or "You keep messing up," recognize that those whispers are words of condemnation and not God's voice. You can shut down condemning words with

God's truth by saying, "Thank You, God, for loving me and forgiving me. I am worthy of Your love and generous blessings."

Prayer

Dear God, I come humbly before You to confess _____. I know that I have not trusted You but have decided to make my own way. God, I want to be honest before You because I know that my sin does impact others, whether I can see it or not. Thank You for 1 John 1:9, which reminds me that when I confess my sin to You, You are faithful to forgive me of my sin and cleanse me of unrighteousness. Thank You, God. In Jesus' name, Amen.

DAY 3: CHANGING THE CHANNEL

As a Christian, I know that God loves me unconditionally and that my salvation is sure because of Christ, but sometimes I still get mad at myself when I mess up the things I want so desperately to get right. Like not worrying.

Though I don't worry as much as I used to, I wish I never battled worry; but it seems to come so easily, especially when it has to do with my family, friends, and finances. You know something I don't ever worry about? The red notification bubbles on my phone. My home screen has so many red bubbles that it looks like it has the measles. When I shared a screenshot of it on social media, it sent a number of people into a panicked frenzy!

I wish I didn't worry about certain parts of my life just as I don't waste a worry on those notifications. I would like to be able to pray and ask God to remove all of my worries, and then not worry anymore. But here's what I'm learning: When we battle worry, we do more than just eliminate a worry. Battling worry can be a powerful form of worship. What do I mean? Worship is expressing our love and devotion to God. When we see the worry battle as an opportunity to worship God by making Him bigger in our lives, it changes our perspective. It's like changing the channel from WorryFlix to FaithFlix.

Today we're going learn how we can change the channel in our lives by enlisting the help of three fighting friends: Peace, Courage, and Strength. They are Spirit-empowered soldiers that position us before God's sovereignty and power. These fighting friends have helped me "change the channel" in my own life. Though I'm not 100 percent worry free, I no longer get stuck on it. Worry used to overpower me and make me weak, but enlisting my fighting friends has built my faith muscles and stamina.

Rather than feeling guilty for having worries, let's change the channel and see our fight as an opportunity to worship God and grow in faith. Our fighting friends will help get us there! Let's get to know each one.

Fighting Friend #1: Peace

Our first fighting friend is Peace, which comes to us through God's powerful words of assurance and security. You know that you're at peace when you're calm, even if chaos is happening around you. Peace begins with God.

After the Israelites' defeat at Ai, God speaks again to Joshua:

> Then the LORD said to Joshua, "Do not be afraid or discouraged. Take all your fighting men and attack Ai, for I have given you the king of Ai, his people, his town, and his land."
>
> (Joshua 8:1)

What's the first thing God says to Joshua?

What assurance does God give Joshua?

Put yourself in Joshua's sandals for a moment. After the emotional experiences in the Valley of Achor and at Ai, Joshua's feelings might be all over the board. Yes, he has faith, but God wants to give him a very important reminder.

The words "Do not be afraid or discouraged" must feel like a hug around Joshua's soul. God is renewing the promise He made to Joshua before the first battle at Jericho was fought. Even after tough times, God hasn't changed the plan, and He reassures Joshua that He is still in charge.

I can imagine Joshua tilting his head, closing his eyes, taking a deep breath, and relaxing. That's peace!

In the New Testament, Jesus speaks about peace in the face of uncertainty and fear.

Read John 14:27 in the margin. How does Jesus describe peace?

"I am leaving you with a gift—peace of mind and heart. And the peace I give is a gift the world cannot give. So don't be troubled or afraid."

(John 14:27)

Jesus knows that the disciples are dealing with tremendous uncertainty about the future. They don't understand what it will mean for Him to be taken from them. They don't know what Jesus' departure will mean for their group. What if the religious leaders who threatened Jesus continue to pursue them? With all of these worries swirling around in the disciples' hearts and minds, Jesus knows exactly what they need.

Why do you think Jesus describes peace as a gift?

In a world where bad things happen, including to good people, it's easy for us to feel like we're living on pins and needles, just waiting for something bad to happen to us. But when we have Jesus' gift of peace, we realize that we're calm, even in our chaotic world. I love how Andy Stanley describes the power of peace in our lives. He basically says that if you have peace, you're happy, because happy people have peace; but if you don't have peace, then "no-thing" will make you happy.[9]

How would you describe the difference between the peace that Jesus gives and the kind of peace you've tried to find on your own?

Jesus' gift of peace is just one of the many blessings we receive as children of God. If you've accepted Jesus as your Savior and Lord, then Jesus' gift of peace is for you! When peace begins to grow in your life, you'll discover that nothing can compare to the assurance of knowing that you're always secure and unconditionally loved by God.

How much we experience our fighting friend of Peace directly correlates to how much time we spend learning and applying God's promises in our lives. I've found that my level of peace is connected to how often I memorize and meditate on God's promises. If you want more of God's peace in your life, then memorize and meditate on more of God's promises. Later this week, you'll do an exercise that trains you to get into the habit of meditating on God's promises.

> **If you want more of God's peace in your life, then memorize and meditate on more of God's promises.**

Fighting Friend #2: Courage

Our second fighting friend is Courage. Many have said, "Courage is fear that has said its prayers." Courage isn't acting without fear but a passionate commitment to act even when afraid. While Joshua never says that he is afraid, God begins the pre-battle instructions with a familiar phrase:

> [1]Then the LORD said to Joshua, "Do not be afraid or discouraged. Take all your fighting men and attack Ai, for I have given you the king of Ai, his people, his town, and his land. [2]You will destroy them as you destroyed Jericho and its king. But this time you may keep the plunder and the livestock for yourselves. Set an ambush behind the town."

³So Joshua and all the fighting men set out to attack Ai. Joshua chose 30,000 of his best warriors and sent them out at night ⁴with these orders: "Hide in ambush close behind the town and be ready for action."

(Joshua 8:1-4)

How many fighting men does God tell Joshua to take with him into battle? (v. 3)

This time, Joshua follows God's instructions and takes all of the fighting men into battle—all 30,000 of them. He commits his entire army to the task of fighting. Every man is 100 percent in.

In addition to not being afraid, God also tells Joshua to not be

_____.

Again and again God has reminded Joshua to be strong and courageous. But this time God tells him not to be discouraged. Why would God switch the language?

Discouraged means "to deprive one's self of courage or hope."[10] Notice the first three letters, *dis*. The prefix *dis-* means "away [from], apart."[11] Do you think that Joshua might have felt a little separated from his courage after the defeat at Ai? No doubt!

When we're discouraged, we want to give up. Discouragement wants us to believe that failure is imminent and we should give up before it's too late. Discouragement also keeps us from the fight, because we don't believe that whatever we've got to offer will make a difference.

Is there a situation in your life that is discouraging to you right now? If so, describe it briefly.

How do we replace discouragement with courage? First, we get honest with God: "God, I'm afraid that I can't handle this situation, but I believe that You are with me and for me. I might be nervous and shaking, but I trust in You, so I'm not stopping." Second, we take the next wise step, even if we're afraid to take it. In Joshua's case, he stepped into his role as the military leader of the Israelites and excuted that role.

Read Joshua 8:10-17. What did Joshua do to surprise the king of Ai and his army?

Joshua's military execution was pretty amazing! We may not know how Joshua felt, but we do know that even if Joshua was afraid, he still engaged in the fight.

Have you ever heard of the phrase "do it scared"? In her *Make Your Move* Bible study, author Lynn Cowell tells a story of how God prompted her to invite someone to church. She talks about all of her fears, excuses, and even a question: "How am I going to do this, God?" But she kept moving forward and extended the invitation. She writes, "With my heart pounding and with the Lord's help, I asked Johnny if he had found a church yet. As I blurted out my question, I stuck out my church's pen. Johnny looked at the pen. He looked at me. Then, as a dam breaking from flood waters, he poured out his heart. . . . I was stunned. To think I had almost missed this opportunity because I didn't want to do it scared."[12]

Where do you need to step out and "do it scared"? My friend, don't let fear trick you into believing that ignoring the problem or running away from it is the better, safer route. Jon Bloom makes a unique observation about courage that is so applicable to our worry battle: "Courage is not an autonomous, self-generated virtue. Courage is always produced by faith, whether our faith is in God or something else. Courage is a derivative virtue."[13]

Your courage—whether big or small, growing or shrinking—is fueled by your faith. So, when it comes to your worry battle, your courage increases as your trust in God increases.

Think about the situation that is discouraging you right now. Can you identify one or two courageous moves that you can make in that situation?

Are there any lingering fears that you have? If so, list them here and pray over them now:

For me, there are some people in my family who do not know Jesus. I can get discouraged when I hear about hardship or heartache in their lives because I love and care about them so much. I've worried about their children and their

> Your courage . . . is fueled by your faith.

Extra Insight

Everything – Jesus = Nothing

Jesus + Nothing = Everything[14]
— Mark Batterson

health as well as their eternal destiny. And in those times when I've wimped out and missed an opportunity to talk to them about Jesus, I've been discouraged by that, too. Like Joshua, I need to omit the "dis" from discourage and ride my courage off toward what God has called me to say and do in their lives. I love these words of Mark Batterson: "When you have a setback, you do not take a step back, because God is already preparing your comeback."[16] When we put our trust in God, we have the courage we need to face whatever is before us.

Fighting Friend #3: Strength

One of the earliest songs I learned as a kid was "Jesus Loves Me." There's a line in that song that goes, "Little ones to him belong, they are weak but he is strong." Even though I learned that song as a kid, I'm still singing that song as an adult. There are many times when life kicks my behind, and I desparately need God's strength to make it through the day.

Our third and final fighting friend is Strength. This fighting friend helps us keep hanging on and holding on for as long as the battle rages in our life. As we're about to see, Joshua's strength is tested after God gives him a specific command as the Israelites fight:

> [18]Then the LORD said to Joshua, "Point the spear in your hand toward Ai, for I will hand the town over to you." Joshua did as he was commanded. [19]As soon as Joshua gave this signal, all the men in ambush jumped up from their position and poured into the town. They quickly captured it and set it on fire....
>
> [21]When Joshua and all the other Israelites saw that the ambush had succeeded and that smoke was rising from the town, they turned and attacked the men of Ai. [22]Meanwhile, the Israelites who were inside the town came out and attacked the enemy from the rear. So the men of Ai were caught in the middle, with Israelite fighters on both sides. Israel attacked them, and not a single person survived or escaped....
>
> [26]For Joshua kept holding out his spear until everyone who had lived in Ai was completely destroyed.
>
> (Joshua 8:18-19, 21-22, 26)

How long did Joshua hold out his spear?

In this scene, God commands Joshua to hold his spear toward Ai until the Israelite army destroys the city and its people. The raised spear is not only a cue for the ambush to begin but also a signal for the main army to turn from their retreat and fight.

Similar to the way that Moses held up his hands years before, Joshua holds up his spear until the twelve thousand enemy soldiers and all of the people of

Ai are wiped out (except the king). We don't know how long his arm is in the air, but we do know that he does not give up or quit.

Often we think about strength only in physical terms, such as how much weight we can lift or how many reps we can do. Physical strength can be seen and measured, but we forget that spiritual and emotional strength are also observable.

When I think about spiritual strength, I remember my friend Sue. The last time I saw Sue was the day before she went to be with Jesus. Sue battled cancer for more than seven years. A former oncology nurse, she fought to stay with her children and grandchildren as long as she could. On a visit with Sue the spring before she died, she told me that she was running out of experimental medicine trials. I went home and wrote out a card for my prayer closet, asking God to show His mercy and grace in her life.

On my last visit to see Sue at her home, her hospital bed occupied the entire left side of the living room. She was asleep, and her husband asked if I wanted him to wake her. Instead, I asked if I could just sit and pray for her. After a few minutes of praying, Sue woke up.

It was such a privilege to look into the eyes of a woman who kept her eyes on Jesus as she fought with cancer and experienced the loss of health insurance, life insurance, and employment. At her memorial service, one of Sue's daughters called her "The Warrior Queen," and others described her as a bedrock—such powerful words for a woman who carried death in her body yet lived full of life.

Think of a woman you know who is spiritually strong. How would you describe her strength?

Read Romans 5:3-4 in the margin. Usually we worry about our struggles, but according to these verses, how does God use our struggles in a positive way in our lives?

Read Ephesians 6:10 in the margin. *How* are we to be strong?

[3] We can rejoice, too, when we run into problems and trials, for we know that they help us develop endurance. [4] And endurance develops strength of character, and character strengthens our confident hope of salvation.
(Romans 5:3-4)

Finally, be strong in the Lord and in the strength of his might.
(Ephesians 6:10 ESV)

Look up Philippians 4:13 and write it below:

What does Paul say is his source of strength?

Philippians 4:13 is one of our go-to verses on the topic of strength. We often quote it when we're getting geared up for a challenge, a sporting event, a ministry season, or even a treatment for a physical illness. Yet when we look at the verses preceding this one, we see that Paul sheds some light on why he needs Christ's strength.

Read Philippians 4:11-12. What do these verses tell us that Paul has learned?

In verses 11 and 12, Paul shares that he has learned how to be content in every circumstance—whether being hungry or full, whether having his needs met or suffering. We know from other writings of Paul that he had been beaten, stoned, imprisoned, shipwrecked, and more. So here Paul is not praying for strength to survive difficult things. He has already survived them! Paul needs strength to be content, not to perform.

The Greek word for "strength" in Philippians 4:13 is *endunamoó*.[19] It is the combination of two words: en,[20] meaning "with," and *dunamoó*,[21] which means "to make strong." It's where our word *dynamite* comes from. So, the strength that comes from God is powerful!

You know that you're living in God's powerful strength when you thrive in the midst of uncertainty. Even as you don't know what tomorrow holds, your heart, mind, and soul are fully engaged in God's purpose for your life. Your circumstances might be uncertain, but you still know and live God's purpose for you. That's living by God power!

Can you recall a time in your life when you knew that Christ's strength was carrying you through a difficult situation? If so, describe it briefly:

> You know that you're living in God's powerful strength when you thrive in the midst of uncertainty.

As we wrap up today's study and you think about the three fighting friends who empower you to move from fighting in fear to fighting in faith, which of the fighting friends do you need to activate more often in your worry battle? You might find that you've got a natural preference for one or two of your fighting friends; but as we'll learn in tomorrow's study, we've got to train all three if we want to fight fiercely in faith.

Apply It: Wisdom Wednesday

"When a man has no strength, if he leans on God, he becomes powerful."

—D. L. Moody[22]

Prayer

Dear God, I can't fight worry on my own, and I want to be in position for Your power to bring me victory. I am grateful that You speak the same words to me that You did to Joshua. I don't have to be afraid or discouraged because You've given me the fighting friends of Peace, Courage, and Strength to help me fight life's battles in faith. Thank You! In Jesus' name, Amen.

DAY 4: POSITIONED FOR GOD'S POWER

I don't love to work out. It's not that I don't like to work out; it's just that I don't love it. Working out requires that I choose to make myself uncomfortable. When I work out, I must move my body in a manner that is inconsistent with happily lounging on my sofa. As I'm twisting, kicking, or stretching, I cannot eat cookies, peanut butter, chocolate-dipped anything, or ice cream. Sweating salty droplets of water is not the same as floating on a raft in a swimming pool. For me, a workout always represents the opposite of what I'd rather be doing. However, for all of my complaining, I still work out. Why? Because I love you. That may sound sappy or strange, but it's 100 percent true.

You see, I realized that if I am to follow God's call on my life to serve others, then I have to follow His call to prepare for that service by making sure that I stay as healthy as possible. In his book *The Coaching Habit*, coach Michael Bungay Stanier shares a story from author Leo Babauta, who teaches that we are most successful in establishing a new habit when we tie our commitment to serving others.[23] So, I love you, therefore, I work out.

Read 1 Timothy 4:8 in the margin. Why is training for godliness even better than physical training?

Today's Takeaway

When my fighting friends are on my side, God's victory in my worry battle is never far behind!

Physical training is good, but training for godliness is much better, promising benefits in this life and in the life to come.

(1 Timothy 4:8)

Living the life God intends for us, which includes being victorious over worry, requires training. So, in order to battle worry we need to establish some new "work out" habits. There are some skills that can help us get into position for God's power to crush our worry. Our fighting friends that we met yesterday— Peace, Courage, and Strength—need a training regimen so they will be prepared for battle when we need them most. If we don't work them out, then worry will wear us out!

Let's walk through this training regimen together.

1. Practicing Peace by Meditating on God's Promises

Meditating on Scripture is a discipline of the Christian life that we know we should practice, but we often think we don't have the time. We want to just read our Bibles, check that off our list, and move on. But the importance of this training tool is highlighted by God at the beginning of the Book of Joshua.

Underline the words *meditate* and *recite* in the different translations of Joshua 1:8 below:

> *Study this Book of Instruction continually. Meditate on it day and night. (NLT)*

> *Keep this Book of the Law always on your lips; meditate on it day and night. (NIV)*

> *Never stop speaking about this Instruction scroll. Recite it day and night. (CEB)*

In Joshua's time, the people didn't have multiple Bibles in their homes or on their smartphones. The way that they communicated Scripture was by memorizing and reciting it orally. The Hebrew word for "meditate" and "recite" in this verse is *hagah* (pronounced daw-gaw).[25] It means essentially "to ponder continually." When we ponder continually, we have an increased connection and understanding of whatever we ponder.

Read Hebrews 10:23 in the margin. What does this verse tell us about who God is and why we can put our trust and hope in Him?

Let us hold fast the confession of our hope without wavering, for he who promised is faithful.
(Hebrews 10:23 ESV)

Now read Psalm 119:11. What is the purpose of hiding God's Word in our hearts?

I have hidden your word in my heart,
   that I might not sin against you.
       (Psalm 119:11)

We want to hold on to God's promises because God will be faithful to fulfill them; and the outcome is avoiding sin—including worry. It has been said that 85 percent of the things we worry about will never happen.[26] So rather than allow our minds to drift toward angst-inducing worry about things that have an 85 percent chance of never happening, let's focus on blessings that we know 100 percent will happen. It's ironic, isn't it, that we spend so much mental energy and time worrying and yet we're intimidated by spending time memorizing Scripture.

What do you think would happen if you were to meditate on one of God's promises every time you noticed yourself worrying? Explain your response.

I love this quotation from pastor John Ortberg: "Meditation is not a confusing activity. In a sense, meditation is just positive worry. If you know how to worry, you know how to mediate."[27]

Here's an opportunity for you to practice meditation today.

Pocket Promises

Step 1: Choose one of the following Scriptures for this exercise, and write the verse on an index card or a small note card or sticky note.

Psalm 4:8; Psalm 56:3; Isaiah 26:3; Matthew 6:33; 2 Thessalonians 3:3

Step 2: Begin meditating on the verse by answering the following questions:

What is God's promise to me?

How will believing this promise give me peace?

Extra Insight

A popular proverb often attributed to Ralph Waldo Emerson says, "We are what we think about all day long."

Extra Insight

Tim Keller identifies three outcomes of meditation:

1. Meditation promises stability.

2. Meditation promises character and substance.

3. Meditation promises blessedness.[28]

Worry doesn't have a chance against prayer!

How will today be different if I believe this promise of God?

Step 3: Put your Scripture card in your pocket, purse, or cell phone case. Take it out periodically throughout the day and work on memorizing it.

___ **Check when done.**

Step 4: Through this experience, how has God deepened your understanding of this promise to you? Write your observations below:

2. Practicing Courage through Prayer

Most of us pray, but what does it mean to practice the regular habit or discipline of prayer, and how can that be a training regimen for our fighting friend Courage?

First, prayer is the tool that creates a hostile territory for worry to enter. In other words, worry doesn't have a chance against prayer! In her book *Fervent*, Priscilla Shirer says that prayer is the fight of our lives against a very real enemy. She writes, "[The enemy] might keep coming, but he won't have victory anymore. Because it all starts failing when we start praying."[29]

Courage is the action step of our prayers. When we pray to God, He fills us with His truth, promises, and power. This means that prayer is the fuel line that funnels God's power into our courage tank. It's been said that life is a marathon, and if that's the case, then we need sufficient prayers to fill our courage tank. Unfortunately, our prayer lives often do not have enough gas to get us to the store and back. If we want full-on courage, then we need a disciplined prayer life defined by the following qualities:

- **Focus:** Do my prayers reflect God's priorities? (Matthew 6:9-13)
- **Persistence:** Am I faithful in praying for even the most difficult situations? (1 Thessalonians 5:17)
- **Consistency:** Do I make space in my life each day to disengage from the world and engage fully in prayer so that my mind may be transformed? (Romans 12:2)

How would you describe your current practice or discipline of prayer? What do you sense God calling you to do differently, If anything?

3. Practicing Strength with the Power of Obedience

Just as we won't build our physical strength unless we do weight-bearing exercises, we won't build our spiritual strength unless we hold on to faith when we're stressed or suffering. There's a "yes" under stress that strengthens us, and it's a yes to God's commands. In fact, saying "yes" to God's commands is the best way to flex our faith muscle. When we say "yes" to God, we get to see God's faithfulness to us, and that strengthens our faith. Obedience is the conduit through which the power of the Holy Spirit flows into our lives.

John Ortberg explains it this way: "Our job is to be ruthless about saying yes when we believe God is speaking to us. Every time we do, we will get a little more...receptive, a little more tuned in to God's channel. On the other hand, when we say, 'no, I'd rather stay in my aisle seat,' we make ourselves a little less likely to hear him in the future."[30]

Read Joshua 1:8 in the margin. What does God promise will be the result if Joshua is obedient?

God promises Joshua success if he obeys God's commands. But God's yardstick for success looks much different than ours, requiring obedience in all circumstances. Winning our battle over worry requires obedience to God's leadings even when we're under tremendous pressure. But obedience is a workout that literally works worry out of our lives!

Read Isaiah 46:3-4. What does God say that He will do?

How does this encourage you to practice obedience?

This Book of the Law shall not depart from your mouth, but you shall meditate on it day and night, so that you may be careful to do according to all that is written in it. For then you will make your way prosperous, and then you will have good success.

(Joshua 1:8 ESV)

Think about the situations that you've been worrying about. What opportunities do you have to practice obedience to God in those situations?

When we're strong spiritually, we're dangerous to the forces of evil. In fact, as we become stronger and worry begins to fall away, we can expect the enemy of our souls to up the ante in our lives. But that just gives us an opportunity to obey God into greater strength, and we do that by saying yes to God!

You might be wondering, "How do I know if God wants me to say yes to something?" If you know that the Bible calls us to do something, then do it without waiting for God to impress it upon your heart. If you need to forgive, then engage in the forgiveness process. If you need to step up and use your gifts to serve, then by all means, sign up. If you feel prompted to do something and it doesn't conflict with the Bible, then do it anyway. My faith in God grows every time I say yes to His leading.

I hope that you've been challenged and equipped with practical ways to train your fighting friends. Remember, the more we train our fighting friends, the more we'll be positioned to experience God's victory. Every moment you spend training your fighting friends will be to your benefit!

Apply It: Temperature Check Thursday

How are you doing? Take a moment to honestly assess where you are in your worry battle.

Circle the number that indicates where you are today:

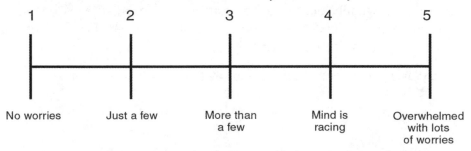

1	2	3	4	5
No worries	Just a few	More than a few	Mind is racing	Overwhelmed with lots of worries

If you circled a 1 or 2, what's helping you to keep worry on a low level?

If you circled a 3, 4, or 5, why do you think you're struggling?

Review the tools and spiritual disciplines we've learned so far. What do you want to try—or retry—in order to get in position to experience God's victory?

Prayer

Dear God, thank You for the fighting friends that You've given me. I need the peace, courage, and strength that only You can provide as I battle against my fears and worries today. God, I trust in You, and I am confident that, whatever I face, You'll be by my side. I know that every "yes" I say to You draws me closer to You and to victory. In Jesus' name, Amen.

This week we have been journeying with the Israelites during a very difficult and worry-filled season of their early days in Canaan. They were doing great after Jericho and then, bam! Someone committed a sin, and the Israelites experienced a setback followed by a meltdown before God got them back on track to experience victory. If you feel like your life follows that same kind of rhythm, my hope is that you've discovered you aren't alone. I've seen that up-and-down rhythm in my life, too. Rather than be discouraged, we can follow in the footsteps of Joshua after God told him to "get up!" Both he and the Israelites had a period of self-examination, confession, and repentance, and then they resumed the work God called them to do.

Today we're going to go one step further and learn about a secret weapon we can use to help us in periods of self-examination as well as times when we need to get up and get moving in God's power. We use the term "secret weapon" to describe a person or thing that surprises the enemy. Secret weapons have the power to radically shift the trajectory of the struggle, swinging momentum back toward the one with the secret weapon.

The secret weapon we're going to learn about today is a spiritual discipline that many Christians neglect to practice on a regular basis. As a longtime Christ-follower, I actually resisted this discipline because I just didn't want to do it. Yet it has been a game-changer in my faith on many levels. This secret weapon is fasting.

Today's Takeaway

When I practice worry, I get weaker; but when I practice the promises of God, He gives me power. And when I remember what God says, I forget how to worry!

What do you think or feel about fasting? Circle the answer that best matches your response:

I don't know much about it.

I'm intimidated by it/uncomfortable with it.

I've tried fasting, and it was not a good experience.

I've fasted in the past, but it has been a while.

I engage in periodic or regular fasting.

Turn to Matthew 4 and read verses 1-4. How long did Jesus fast?

According to verse 2, what effect did the fasting have on Jesus?

Jesus began His ministry in the wilderness that stretched for miles from the Jordan Valley west toward Jerusalem. Then and now, there are no comforts in the desert—no soft pillows or beds, no friends to share the experience. Instead, there is only arid terrain and desert animals foraging for water and food. The desert is a place of extremes: extreme temperatures, extreme loneliness, extreme hunger.

Since Jesus was fully God and fully man, He experienced the same physical effects of fasting that we do; and His experience was meant to be an example for us. The Holy Spirit actually led Jesus into the wilderness where He fasted and then was tempted so that we could see how the power of God living within us can help us overcome human desires that can get out of control.

The devil knew that Jesus had been fasting and came to tempt Him.

According to Matthew 4:3, when did the devil come, and what suggestion did he make to Jesus?

We don't know at what point the devil showed up during Jesus' forty-day fast, but my guess is that he probably waited until Jesus was at his hungriest. So we can be sure that the devil wasn't trying to convince Jesus to turn those stones into stale, three-day-old bread. No, the temptation was for Jesus to turn the stones into soft, delicious loaves of yeasty goodness—perhaps with a little butter on the side!

Write below Jesus' reply found in verse 4:

As a woman who has dealt with emotional eating in my past as a way of coping with stress and worry, Jesus' words in verse 4 minister to my soul. For many years, snacks smoothed over my worries and struggle. It took fasting to help me see that I had shifted my desire for comfort, ease, and peace to food instead of to deeper faith in God. Richard Foster sums it up so well: "More than any other Discipline, fasting reveals the things that control us."[31]

When it comes to our worry battle, fasting is a secret weapon because it puts us in position for God to do deep work in our hearts, minds, and souls— where much of the worry we face is rooted. Fasting is a tool that God uses to dig up the dirtiest, crustiest roots of our worry.

Foster continues his explanation of the purpose of fasting and how it reveals our truest self with these insightful words:

> We cover up what is inside us with food and other good things, but in fasting these things surface. If pride controls us, it will be revealed almost immediately....Anger, bitterness, jealousy, strife, fear—if they are within us, they will surface during fasting. At first, we will rationalize that our anger is due to our hunger; then we will realize that we are angry because the spirit of anger is within us. We can rejoice in this knowledge because we know that healing is available through the power of Christ.[32]

I've experienced revelation through fasting in my own life. For the past few years, I've followed God's call for me to engage in a weekly fast. In the months before I began the fast, I really struggled with the idea, because I like food. Scratch that, I love food. The thought of giving up food one day a week seemed like a punishment rather than a place for God to do deep work in my life. But then a situation happened in my family that opened the door to a season of great pain and heartache. I knew that I would not survive that season of my life without more of God and less of me. That's when fasting shifted from an invitation to an imperative in my life. And through this discipline, God not only has revealed Himself and answered prayers but also has shown me deep truth about the condition and needs of my heart. In many ways, my weekly fast helps me train for adversity in the Christian life. As I surrender my preferences for a day, I'm strengthened against problem areas that used to create conflict in my life. I have found that when I fast, I'm better able to hold my tongue, refrain from being impulsive, and greatly reduce emotional eating.

This weekly fast has been so beneficial in my life that I continue it to this day. The fast begins on Tuesday after dinner and ends with breakfast on

Thursday. I refrain from solid foods and drink tea, juice, broth, or the occasional cup of coffee. Generally, I arrange my schedule around my fast so that I do not bring public attention to it.

On my fast day, I still make meals for my family and conduct my business. So, in these ways it's no different than other days of the week. However, it's the day of the week when I can count on the devil showing up, as he did with Jesus in the wilderness, to tempt me and whisper worries.

If you have fasted in the past or currently practice the discipline of fasting, what have been some of the challenges you have experienced?

If fasting is a new or untried practice for you, what are some of your concerns about fasting?

One concern some Christians express about fasting is that they are not "spiritual enough" for it. They often cite Matthew 6:16 as a reason to leave fasting in the closet, so to speak, as a tool to be used only by select, more spiritual Christians.

Read Matthew 6:17-18. Are all believers supposed to fast? What phrase clues us into Jesus' answer?

Jesus uses the phrase "When you fast . . ." to signify that all believers should be fasting at some point. As I've mentioned, learning to practice this new habit has been a significant spiritual journey for me, but it has helped me keep my heart turned toward God and open to His presence and voice in a profound way.

There are two points I'd like to make related to these verses. First, Jesus is condemning the motive of the Pharisees, not censoring our freedom to discuss fasting during our spiritual discussions with one another. Though we're not to use fasting as a way to make others think that we're spiritually superior, others might have the courage to fast if they knew that we are doing it, too.

Second, the Pharisees in Jesus' time used fasting as a public way to draw attention to themselves. They wanted people to see them "wasting away" as a symbol that they were uber spiritual. That type of fasting doesn't honor God. Neither does fasting with the attitude that by giving up meals or something else, God will give you what you want. Instead, fasting is a secret way to draw

close to God and do deep spiritual work. And when it comes to the worry battle, fasting is our secret weapon to blast longtime, stubborn, hard-to-move worry from our lives.

Campus Crusade founder Bill Bright wrote a guide that offers not only spiritual insights related to fasting but also many practical helps. Drawing on that classic guide, which includes seven steps, I'd like to offer a very simple, three-step process: plan, prepare, and pray.[33] My challenge to you is to pick one day in the next week to fast following this process.

Step 1: PLAN (Identify why you are fasting.)

Put a check mark beside the reason or objective for fasting that is most applicable in your life right now:

I need . . .

_____ **spiritual renewal**

_____ **guidance**

_____ **healing**

_____ **resolution of a problem**

_____ **grace to handle a difficult situation**

Identifying the reason or objective for your fast will help give you focus and guidance as you pray.

Step 2: PREPARE (Choose the type and duration of fast.)

To get your feet wet in the discipline of fasting, you might choose to eliminate one meal and drink liquids instead. (If you have any concerns about medical issues and risks, speak with your healthcare provider.) Or you might simply omit a particular kind of food or an activity for a period of time, beginning with one hour or one day.

The principle of fasting is surrendering a habit in order to make a spiritual connection with God. Whatever you choose to fast from should be a regular habit so that when you fast, you will notice that your entire way of life is following a different rhythm. Your fasting goal should be to increase your connection with God, as well as to strengthen your spiritual sensitivity; it is not a means to impress God or to try to gain favor.

In his fasting guide, Bright mentions all types of fasts from digital fasts (unplugging from connected devices for a period) through forty-day water-only fasts. The ultimate decision for the type and duration of your fast should come from conviction born in prayer. If prayer doesn't provide clarity, talk about it with a trusted Christian friend.

Today's Takeaway

Fasting is a secret weapon that puts me in position for God to dig up the roots of my worry.

Step 3: PRAY (Focus strategically on God.)

It's important to have an intentional plan for prayer during fasting. Someone told me years ago that if you fast without praying, then you're just going hungry. After all, prayer is really the point of fasting.

My own strategy is to replace the meal, or whatever I've surrenderd, with prayer. You can still participate in family or shared meals by having a cup of water or coffee. Prayer time can take place either before or after the meal. During my fast day, I like to pray for a time period equivalent to the duration of my meal. Sometimes that prayer time includes listening to worship music. My objective is focusing on God more than on what I want or need, even though I do pray about that as well.

You will experience hunger during a fast, but you can get through it. As one who loves food, I've had to learn to talk to my hunger pangs and remind my body that the fast is just one day. If something happens to interrupt my day, such as an unexpected business luncheon, I simply determine whether it is prudent to contine the fast or to temporarily break it. Again, fasting is a discipline, not a guarantee or an activity to gain God's favor.

One of the primary benefits of praying during a fast is that you are more aware of your dependence on God and, consequently, are more likely to pray raw, honest, heartfelt prayers. And that's exactly how God wants us to come to Him!

Apply It: Freedom Friday

This week we've been exploring how to use our fighting friends to battle back after a defeat and subsequent spiritual meltdown. Recall a time when you experienced a setback—whether in the past or recently, perhaps even this week.

What is the most valuable thing you've learned this week that will help you get back on track after a setback and experience victory?

Prayer

Dear God, I am so grateful for Your love for me, for all that You've aleady done in my life, and for all You're doing now to help me win the battle over worry. This week You've challenged me to get serious about meditation on Your Word, prayer, obedience, and fasting. Lord, these things are not always easy, so I ask You to help me put them into practice. I want to position myself to receive Your power to win over worry and every other struggle in my life. I'm thanking You in advance for victory! In Jesus' name, Amen.

Proverbs 12:25—*Worry weighs down; encouragement cheers up*

1. Peace—The _____ that we need

2. Courage—Passionate _____

3. Strength—What _____ us to keep holding on and hanging on

Joshua 1:8—*Study, Mediate, Obey*

1. _____ this Book continually.

2. _____ on it day and night.

3. _____ everything written in it.

It's _____ who brings us the victory.

Joshua 5:13-14—*The Lord's Commander Confronts Joshua*

1 Samuel 17:32, 45—*David and Goliath*

Ephesians 1:19-20—*God's power for those who believe*

You may not have strength to carry on, but God has strength to _____ _____.

DEFEATING THE KINGS OF WORRY

Attacking the Roots of Our Worries

Joshua 9–11

MEMORY VERSE

"Do not be afraid; do not be discouraged. Be strong and courageous. This is what the Lord will do to all the enemies you are going to fight."

(Joshua 10:25 NIV)

This week Joshua and the Israelites encounter a wave of new enemies. Until now the Israelites have battled one king and one army at a time. However, we're about to see what happens when fear compels a group of Canaanite kings—who likely fought each other at times—to form an alliance against the Israelites.

In some ways, I appreciate how God gave Joshua and the Israelites a couple of one-on-one warm-up battles against Jericho and Ai before having them face multiple kings at once. Just as one king respresents a certain level of power, a cohort of kings represents an exponential increase in power and capacity. Joshua might have been overwhelmed if he had not kept his heart and mind on God's plans and promises.

Do you ever feel overwhelmed when many big issues crowd into your life all at once? Futhermore, do you ever feel that some of those issues do not get resolved before new issues pile on? (I have a feeling that you are nodding your head right now.) When I look at my Wheel of Worry (look back at page 33 for a refresher), there have been times in my life when multiple big worries took over my life.

But there's hope! I love that the Bible is filled with stories of regular people like you and me who face off against situations and circumstances bigger than our ability to overcome. People like to say that God doesn't give us more than we can handle. I disagree with that statement. I believe that life regularly gives us more than we can handle so that we realize our need for God, who can handle it all! That's why the definition of victory in this study is so meaningful. Victory is when we believe that God is with us and for us in every circumstance, real or imagined. Therefore, victory is grounded in God's character, not in our capacity.

Is there an age-old worry that has overshadowed your life? Perhaps you've carried worries over abandonment, financial insecurity, or death of loved ones since your childhood. God can give you victory over even the oldest and deepest worries. Mark 10:27 tells us, "Humanly speaking it is impossible, but not with God. Everything is possible with God." Perhaps you've heard Christians say the phrase "But God." The word *but* is often used as an excuse, but when we put "But God" together, that combination becomes an explanation for the extraordinary. There will never be a king-sized worry or problem that can ever stand against "But God," because the supernatural power that God used to raise Jesus from the dead (Ephesians 1:19-20) is the same supernatural power that God uses to give you victory over whatever king-sized drama is going on in your life.

Throughout the week we're going to step back and look at the roots of some of our worries. Just as the events of the Israelites' conquest were set into motion centuries before them, some of our worrying tendencies are rooted in the experiences of those who came before us, as well as our own past experiences. As we uncover these roots, we will attack them by learning how to tell the difference between an actionable concern and a wasted worry. We'll also be challenged to follow Joshua's example and pray the boldest prayer of

our lives, inviting God to do what we don't have enough time or power to do on our own.

Friend, I'm excited for you, especially if there are some king-size fears and worries that have had power over your life for far too long. In Jesus' name, it's time to take those king-sized worries down!

DAY 1: OUR ROOTS OF WORRY

Last week we saw God lead the Israelites to victory at Ai. Take a moment and put yourself in the shoes of someone who is living in the land of Canaan as news of that victory spreads in the streets. Earlier in our study we pictured ourselves in the Israelite camp, but what about the inhabitants of Canaan? The people occupying the land do not call it the Promised Land; they call it home. Rather than just brush off the inhabitants as nameless, faceless people, it might be helpful for us to understand more about them—especially as a series of great battles for possession of the land begin to unfold.

In Canaan at this time, there are different people groups with different kings ruling over the city-state-like territories, and these individual kings rule under the authority of the king of Hazor, whose kingdom also is in Canaan. The king of Hazor, however, reports to the Egyptian pharaoh. Remember that the Israelites were slaves in Egypt for four hundred years, and the ruling pharaoh did not throw them a bon voyage party when they fled. It's not hard to suppose that Egypt sent word of the Israelites' exodus and movement toward Canaan to the kings living east and west of the Jordan. I wonder if those kings were confused when the Israelites' eleven-day journey dragged out forty years!

Everything we encounter in life has a story with a beginning, middle, and end. Today we're going to look more closely at the backstory of the Israelites and Canaanites. And as the kings are banding together against God's people, we're going to arm ourselves with understanding of the roots of this conflict.

You're also going to take some time to uncover the roots of your own worry. There's a backstory of your worry, too, and today you're going to think about that. Once you know the ties to your past that are holding you back, you can cut them and move into the future.

Read Joshua 9:1-2, and list the Canaanite kings that hear about the Israelites' victory at Ai:

What do they decide to do?

With allegiant ties to the Egyptians,[1] these Canaanite kings likely have not forgotten the events that led up to the Israelites' flight from Egypt. After all, an entire generation of firstborn Egyptian sons was lost upon the Israelites' departure. Joshua surely knows that the Canaanite kings' alliance might be strengthened with additional support from Egypt.

What is happening in the Book of Joshua, then, is actually related to events that occurred centuries before. Let's dig into the backstory.

The Book of Genesis gives us some important details. In Genesis 10, we see that the Canaanite kings and their people descended from Canaan, who was the son of Ham and the grandson of Noah. In the previous chapter, we learn that after the Flood, God commanded Noah to repopulate the earth, not only in people but also in "products." Noah was a "man of the soil" (Genesis 9:20), and he planted a vineyard. One day Noah drank some wine, and his youngest son, Ham, discovered his father unclothed and passed out in the tent. Ham told his two older brothers, Shem and Japheth, about their father's condition, and they grabbed a covering and backed into the tent to lay it over his body without looking. When Noah woke up and found out what had happened, you might say that there was some drama. The entire event unfolds in Genesis 9:20-27.

Look up Genesis 9:25. Who did Noah curse?

Noah was angry that Ham didn't take steps to treat him with respect in a vulnerable moment. Though Ham had multiple sons, Noah issued a curse only on Ham's son Canaan. And this curse was quite severe, because Noah said that Canaan would be "the lowest of slaves" (NIV, NRSV)—" a servant of servants" (ESV, NASB, KJV). Life can never be good if you are the servant of a servant.

It's important to note that this singular story has been the root cause of much misinterpretation, rationalization, and justification in history. For example, the institution of slavery was largely based on the misinterpretation that Ham was cursed, not Canaan. Though the race of Noah and his sons is not described in the Bible, through the centuries Ham came to be widely portrayed as black and the ancestor of dark-skinned peoples; and so the idea of blackness and servitude was linked.[2] Many of those dark-skinned people would be enslaved throughout history because this story was held up as divine justification—even though wrongly so.

Extra Insight

Genesis 10:15-18 also lists people groups that descended from Canaan, with a few differences from the list found in Joshua 9:1-2. The Amorites are the most common people group that descended from Canaan.

When we look closely at Genesis 9, we see that a specific reason why Canaan is cursed instead of his father, Ham, is not given. Commentators propose a few different reasons, but nothing is substantiated in Scripture. We know from Genesis 9:1 that God blessed Noah and his sons after the Flood, so it could be argued that Noah would not have been able to curse Ham after God had blessed him. Others have suggested that Noah might have been making a prophetic pronouncement, seeing Ham's carnal nature in his son Canaan. Or it's possible that the curse was made later, perhaps upon Noah's deathbed, and that Ham was no longer living at that time. In any case, Canaan was the one cursed while Shem and Japheth received praise and blessing.

Read Genesis 9:26-27. Who would Canaan be a slave to?

Noah's curse said that Canaan would be the servant of Shem—and perhaps of Japheth as well, as some translations indicate (NIV, NCV). That may not mean much on face value, but it's important to understand the implication for future generations.

In Genesis 10 and 11, we read about Shem's descendants, and in Genesis 11:26 we read, "After Terah had lived 70 years, he became the father of Abram . . ." (NIV). Here we learn that Abram, later renamed Abraham, was a descendant of Shem. Abraham became the father of Isaac, who was the father of Jacob. And it was Jacob who was renamed Israel and became the forefather of the twelve tribes of Israel. So, we see that the descendants of Shem are the Israelites, and the descendants of Canaan are the Canaanites. The story is getting interesting now, isn't it?

Genesis 10:15-20 explains that, before the time of Abraham, the Canaanites scattered to occupy the areas west of the Jordan River (which we see on our map on page 11). Genesis 10 also identifies the lands where the descendants of Canaan's brothers and cousins spread out to occupy. In Genesis 13, we read how God reaffirmed His promise to give the land of Canaan to Abram, and how Abram came to settle there. Then, in Genesis 15, God explains how Abram's descendants would leave the land, become slaves in a foreign land, and eventually come back to the land of Canaan. At that time, the curse of Canaan spoken by Noah would come to pass.

Read Genesis 15:16 in the margin. How many generations would pass before the sins of the Amorites (descendants of Canaan) would "warrant their destruction" (NLT)?

"After four generations your descendants will return here to this land, for the sins of the Amorites do not yet warrant their destruction."

(Genesis 15:16)

In this four-century delay, we see a foreshadowing of the concept of God's wide mercy. Even though the Amorites rejected God, He did not immediately give them the punishment that they deserved but allowed four generations to pass so that they might turn from their wickedness.

This brings us full circle back to Joshua and the Israelites in Joshua 9. As the Canaanite kings and their armies descend upon the Israelites, they may or may not know about the curse on Canaan's descendants. But even if they do, these kings aren't willing to just give up their land without a fight. More about that tomorrow! For now, let's linger a while longer on God's mercy.

The important backstory we've covered today helps us see how the Israelites' conquest fulfills both the promise of God for a blessing and the fulfillment of righteous judgment in response to sin. Yet even in His response to sin, He shows mercy.

Read Romans 2:4 in the margin. What does this tell us about God's attitude toward our wrongdoing?

Don't you see how wonderfully kind, tolerant, and patient God is with you? Does this mean nothing to you? Can't you see that his kindness is intended to turn you from your sin?
(Romans 2:4)

God is so kind to us! Just as He wanted the Amorites to turn from their sin and return to Him, God wants you and me to turn from our worried-filled, self-centered lives and follow Him. Let's be honest: on our own, we do a lousy job of leading our own lives. That's why we worry! And sin is a major root cause of that worry. Unfortunately, many of us also worry that God may not always be so kind to us. If we're honest, we sometimes worry that God might even punish us for messing up our lives—or at least leave us on our own to pick up the pieces.

How much time have you spent worrying that God is displeased with you? Have you ever avoided God because you were worried that He might require something of you for your mistakes and sins—perhaps even take away someone or something you love? My sweet friend, that is not who God is!

Read 1 Timothy 1:15-16. How does the apostle Paul describe himself?

Look at verse 16. What is the reason Jesus shows patience?

The apostle Paul is writing to a young pastor named Timothy, sharing his story of gratitude for God's mercy. In the previous verses, Paul talks about how he used to blaspheme, and he calls himself the worst of sinners. We all probably have had days when we have felt like Paul and have worried that we are the worst sinner we know.

Look back to 1 Timothy 1:14. What does God pour out abundantly on those who place their faith in Jesus Christ?

As Christ shows you mercy by not giving you the punishment that you deserve, He also lavishly pours out His grace and love on you. That's His heart toward you! My friend, He wants you to stop worrying about your past. That kind of worry is rooted in guilt over sin, but because of Jesus we can have complete confidence in God's great mercy!

Today we've seen that God showed mercy to the Canaanites for generations. You and I are benefactors of that same mercy, too. And best of all, God's mercy for us on this side of the cross has no limits or expiration.

Is there a sin from the past or present that is creating worry in your life? If so, describe that worry below:

Read the following verses, noting what each verse tells you about the past:

Isaiah 43:18 _____

Philippians 3:13-14 _____

2 Corinthians 5:17 _____

According to Ephesians 2:4-7 and 1 Peter 1:3-4, what are we guaranteed because of God's mercy through Jesus Christ?

Read 1 John 1:9 in the margin. What specific guarantee does this verse give us?

But if we confess our sins to him, he is faithful and just to forgive us our sins and to cleanse us from all wickedness.

(1 John 1:9)

Are you ready to let go of worrying about how mistakes of your past might hijack your future? While your mistakes may have messed up some parts of your life, those mistakes are no match for God's power to redeem.

Read Jeremiah 29:11. God knows everything about you, including your past mistakes, yet what does He promise?

Today's Takeaway

I don't have to worry about my past because my mistakes are no match for God's mercy and power to redeem.

Sometimes we rush to get our Bible study done so that we can move on to the next thing. But if you've been struggling with worries about past or present sins, you have an opportunity right now to change the trajectory of your heart and mind. It's time to pray and give it all to God.

Take time to confess your sin, acknowledge your desire to repent (turn away) from your sin, and ask for forgiveness. Then accept God's promise to forgive your sin. If you like, write your prayer or your reflections after prayer below:

Apply It: Monday Motivation

If you've just spoken or written a prayer, how will you live differently as a result? Here's a phrase to remember and repeat to yourself at least once a day this week:

I don't have to worry about my past because God's mercy and forgiveness make me worthy of a blessed future.

Prayer

Gracious God, thank You for Your grace and mercy in my life. I know that I've made mistakes in the past, but I refuse to worry about them because You've promised me a future and a hope. I cancel any worry whispers that try to discourage me from trusting in Your complete forgiveness for me. In Jesus' name, Amen.

DAY 2: SECONDHAND WORRY

One Sunday afternoon I received a message from someone asking for help. This sweet lady, whom I'll call Leah, had just lost her father. If you've lost a parent or any loved one, you know that the grief runs deep. Dealing with grief requires time, rest, and lots of self-care. Yet she was unable to care for herself because she was overwhelmed with worries—except the worries weren't her own. Loved ones in her life had pushed their worries and cares onto her, and she was drowning in them.

I've known Leah almost my entire life. She manages her personal affairs well and plans for the future. Yet in this instance she was ensnared by the uncertainties of her loved ones. I diagnosed Leah's condition as "secondhand worry." Secondhand worry sprouts from the root of control. When we want to manage or fix the affairs of others, we probably will find secondhand worry growing in our hearts.

Secondhand worry is when we suffer the effects of worry because we are trying to carry the load that someone else should be responsible and accountable for managing themselves—whether they be an adult child, spouse, parent, coworker, or friend. We can wear ourselves out with secondhand worry when we do not recognize the difference between worry and concern. It's possible to express care or concern without assuming responsibility for fixing or managing another's affairs. Right now you might be thinking of other terms such as enabling or co-dependency. But those are actually underlying behaviors that contribute to the thinking patterns and feelings of what I'm calling secondhand worry.

Leah told me that she had promised money, time, and energy to help her loved ones get through their situations. She also admitted that this cycle of being stressed out and then bailing others out had been going on for years. In fact, before Leah's father passed away, he gently warned her that taking on others' problems would wear her out. He was right.

If you can relate to Leah, you know that it's a difficult place to be. Life is hard enough trying to fight in faith for our own victory over worry. It's impossible for us to fight someone else's battle, too.

After the Canaanite kings band together, the Israelites find themselves suffering from a case of secondhand worry. As we see what happens when the Israelites ignore God's standing instructions, let's learn from their misfortune and gain some divine wisdom to cure our own secondhand worry.

Read Joshua 9:3-13 and answer the following questions with T (true) or F (false):

_____ 1. The Hivites were the names of the people who lived in Gibeon. (vv. 3, 7)

_____ 2. When the people of Gibeon heard about the Israelite victory, they sent their army to fight Joshua and the men. (v. 4)

_____ 3. A delegation from Gibeon traveled to Gilgal to deceive Joshua and the leaders. (vv. 3-6)

_____ 4. The delegation wanted to make a peace treaty with the Israelites. (v. 6)

_____ 5. They used withered grapes and dried figs as part of their deception. (vv. 4-5)

_____ 6. The delegation told Joshua that they were from a distant country. (v. 6)

Let's imagine the scene. Joshua and his leaders are meeting in tents to plot the next phase of their campaign, and there is a disturbance outside in the camp. As Joshua exits his tent, his soldiers approach him while flanking a group of worn-out-looking travelers. As Joshua inspects the delegation, his eyes notice what the visitors are wearing and carrying. He sees the patched sandals, cracked wineskins, and moldy bread. No doubt the delegation smelled like they'd been traveling for a long time, too.

In verse 7, the Israelites question the delegation and warn them that if the travelers live close by, then a treaty isn't possible. However, the savvy Hivites have come prepared with quite a story.

Read Joshua 9:9-13, and summarize the Hivites' story below:

What is the evidence supporting their explanation?

Can you see the dirty, smelly men eagerly holding up their carefully curated symbols of snookery? Between their props and their story, those men were in the same league as any Academy Award winner for best screenwriter or best screenplay!

Answers: 1. T 2. F 3. T 4. T 5. T 6. T

Unfortunately, the Israelites make a crucial error in what they do next.

Read Joshua 9:14-15. While the Israelites do their due diligence and inspect the evidence, they still miss something very important. What do they neglect to do, and what do they decide to do?

In short, the Israelites neglect to let God lead, and as a result they let what they see in front of them determine their actions, even if those actions conflict with God's previous instructions to them.

Read Exodus 34:11-12 in the margin. What did God tell the Israelites NOT to do? Why?

Write below the first first three words of Exodus 34:11:

_____   _____   _____

What does it mean to listen carefully to God?

[11] "But listen carefully to everything I command you today. Then I will go ahead of you and drive out the Amorites, Canaanites, Hittites, Perizzites, Hivites, and Jebusites.

[12] "Be very careful never to make a treaty with the people who live in the land where you are going. If you do, you will follow their evil ways and be trapped."

(Exodus 34:11-12)

Though God speaks to us in a variety of different ways, there are four common ways we often hear from God:

1. Bible
2. Holy Spirit
3. Other people
4. Circumstances/life experiences (past and present)

God has always spoken in these ways, but in the days before the coming of the Holy Spirit at Pentecost (Acts 2), God often spoke through anointed prophets, priests, and leaders, such as Joshua. In our day, the Holy Spirit lives within every believer to lead us into all truth (John 14:16-17; 16:13-15). Sometimes, we hear people say "I sense" or "I feel" as an indication that they have received a leading from the Holy Spirit to think, feel, or behave a certain way. However, God will never contradict what He has said in His Word. So the Scriptures are our plumb line when it comes to discerning what we think and

feel God is leading us to do. When others indicate they have a leading from God but that leading or the actions following it conflict with God's Word, then that's a huge red flag; and we should pray and seek godly counsel about how to respond.

If God speaks to us in these and other ways, then what does it mean to "listen carefully"? How can we know that we are hearing God? Here's good news: As we train our fighting friends Peace, Courage, and Strength with God's promises, prayer, and the power of obedience, our hearts and minds will be in position to listen to God. In other words, these basic disciplines or habits attune our spiritual ears to hear God's voice.

How does fear or worry get in the way of us listening for God's leading?

Describe a time when worry interfered with your ability to hear from God:

While writing this week's lessons, I began to slide into panic mode as I considered the fast-approaching deadline while trying to prepare for a weekend speaking engagement. My mind began to race as I fretted about all of the undone items on my to-do list. Then I felt God prompt my heart to take a needed walk.

As I put on my walking shoes, I started to meditate on Matthew 6:33 and pray: "God, in this moment I need to see you first. I need to focus my heart, mind, and spirit on You. You said that if I focus on You, that You will order everything else."

I repeated this over and over again as I walked. I actually had to force myself to repeat it in order to force worry out of the door of my heart and mind. You see, I knew that worry had busted in and was starting to attack my fighting friend Peace. I couldn't let Peace go down like that!

As I meditated, my heart rate began to slow, my mind stopped racing, and I could begin to ask God for guidance, praying, "God, show me the way through this busy week."

During my walk, God impressed upon my heart to reset my work schedule after having an erratic schedule for two weeks due to some celebrations and out-of-town guests. Then, God reminded me of a rarely used story in my *Enough Already* book that would make a perfect backdrop story for the message I would be giving that weekend. Finally, God whispered, "Trust me." That was the reminder that I needed for my manuscript deadline.

By the end of my walk, I smiled and celebrated God's victory over the worry I had experienced that morning.

Do you have a story of how you've experienced victory over worry? If so, share it below:

Let's get back to our story of the Israelites, who have an unfortunate revelation that is a direct consequence of not seeking God's leading. After signing the treaty, the Israelites receive some troubling information. Those worn-out looking travelers have come from a nearby territory; they are not a long-distance delegation.

Read Joshua 9:16-18. How long does it take the Israelites to travel from Gilgal to Gibeon?

Why don't the Israelites attack the Hivites in accordance to God's original command? (v. 18)

It's not clear who traveled over three days to visit the Gibeonites and the other cities. A distance of approximately eighty-three miles separated the two cities, so it would have been difficult for the entire Israelite assembly to make the move; but an army could have made it in that time.

Now, the Israelites have made an agreement with people that God specifically commanded them not to make an agreement with. God knew that the practices of the pagan people would infect the hearts and souls of His fast-forgetting people and lead them astray. Just thinking about entering into a treaty with anyone, let alone these people, should have raised a red flag in the mind of Joshua or another Israelite leader. But before we judge Joshua, let's remember that we've done the same kind of thing, too.

When are you most tempted to "wear" or take on someone else's worry?

Is there someone's worry that you are wearing right now? If so, what is it?

Have you ever worried yourself sick or risked your financial security trying to rescue someone who refuses to be responsible for himself or herself?

Just because the Gibeonites try to place their fate in the hands of the Israelites doesn't mean that Joshua and the leaders have to accept responsibility for it. And the same is true for us.

As one who is prone to controlling behaviors, I've had to wake up and take responsibility not for determining the fate of others but for trying to save people that I can't save. Only Jesus saves. Not you and not me. If we don't pay attention to our rescuing behavior, we not only will wear ourselves out with worry but also may send the unintended message that there is no hope for that friend or loved one if we don't step in and "fix" his or her life.

What we want is for them to find the same hope that we have found in Jesus alone. We want our friends and loved ones to enlist the same fighting friends that we have. Most of all, we want those precious people in our lives to get in position to experience the victory that comes from God's power, not our money or our nagging.

I know that this is hard, and you may be struggling with a secondhand worry situation. If so, my heart and prayers go out to you. I encourage you to take that situation to Jesus and stop carrying a load that doesn't belong on your shoulders.

Now, let's take responsibility for what we know we need to change and learn how to apply a new tool in our lives.

Apply It: Tool Tuesday

Sort It Out

Here's a two-part exercise to help you 1) identify those behaviors that assist you in expressing concern and those that reinforce worry, and 2) apply your learnings to a current situation in your life.

Part 1

Mark those emotions and behaviors that demonstrate concern with a "C" and those that demonstrate worry with a "W":

_____ 1. Calling to check on someone

_____ 2. Staying up all night crying

_____ 3. Calling/texting ALL Day

_____ 4. Praying and/or fasting

_____ 5. Listening without giving advice

_____ 6. Getting angry with someone who won't make good decisions

_____ 7. Providing a meal

_____ 8. Giving money you don't have

_____ 9. Nagging

_____ 10. Sending a text or card

_____ 11. Saying "no" to bail out/rescue

_____ 12. Giving a long lecture

Which of these are your first responses when you hear from someone in trouble? Circle them above.

Do you get the same kinds of phone calls or texts from the same people again and again? If so, does this reveal anything to you about your pattern of response? What changes might you need to make?

Part 2

Now apply what you've learned to a situation that is weighing on your heart right now by completing the following chart. The goal is to sort out how to be healthy and helpful instead of becoming infected with secondhand worry, which is dangerous for you and for the other person(s). (See the examples in the margin on the following page.)

Answers: 1. C 2. W 3. W 4. C 5. C 6. W 7. C 8. W 9. W 10. C 11. C 12. W

Name of Person	
Why am I worried about him, her, or them?	
What negative outcome do I fear?	
"Go-To Behaviors" (showing concern)	
"No-Go Behaviors" (reinforcing worry)	

GO-TO BEHAVIORS THAT EXPRESS CONCERN:

Listening without giving advice

Providing a meal

Praying (and fasting) for them

Sending a card

Saying "no" to bail out/rescue

NO-GO BEHAVIORS THAT REINFORCE WORRY:

Staying up all night fretting/crying

Getting angry

Giving money you don't have

Giving money to poor money managers

Long lectures

This tool can be a mental process you walk through whenever you realize you've started to worry, or you may find it helpful to write out your answers so that you can "see" the situation on paper.

Now that you've completed this exercise, what is your next step?

How can you use this tool in the future to help you avoid secondhand worry in your relationships?

Today's Takeaway

When you wear someone else's worry, it will wear you out.

Prayer

Dear God, when I wear someone else's worry, it wears me out! You are big enough for all of us, and I believe that Your promises apply to me and everyone I love and care about. Today I commit to avoid secondhand worry by keeping boundaries on my concern and trusting You through the uncertainty. Amen.

DAY 3: REDEEMING WORRY

Yesterday we were introduced to the Gibeonites. As much as I admire their creativity and storytelling, their deceptive motives sprouted from worry caused by the root of insecurity. We learn from their example that when worry pushes us toward actions that undermine God's promises, the results damage our faith, our relationships, and our future.

Today we're going to see the consequences of the Gibeonites' deception, but we'll also witness a surprising proclamation of faith. You might find some encouragement if worry has ever led you to do the wrong thing.

Read Joshua 9:18-20. What do the Israelite leaders decide to do about the Gibeonites? Why?

Can you picture the Israelite people standing with their arms crossed, giving Joshua and the other leaders the stink eye? As a leader, that probably wasn't Joshua's most popular moment. But let's give the Israelite leaders their due recognition. For a group of people who are prone to wander from God's instructions, there are times when their resolve toward righteousness truly inspires me.

Like me, the Israelites tend to have short memories when it comes to God's instructions; but I'm impressed that they remembered Moses's instructions not to strike treaties with the inhabitants of the land. Joshua and the Israelites thought they had done their due diligence by questioning and examining the strangers, but they later realized that they were deceived; and their sin of entering an agreement without consulting God created a consequence that the entire assembly of Israelites would have to bear. Yet even so, Joshua still acts with honor by upholding the agreement.

Read Joshua 9:21. What, specifically, do Joshua and the leaders decide to do with the Gibeonites?

This is a good strategic solution to a bad situation because the area west of the Jordan is a mountainous territory with many trees, so the Gibeonites will be subject to a lot of necessary, hard labor.

Can you think of a time when you were really worried about something and you did the wrong thing to try to fix it? If so, briefly describe it.

What comes to mind for me is something that happened when I was in my twenties and people began warning me and my husband to buy a house so that we could stop "wasting" money on rent. Looking back on my younger self, I wish that I could tell her to ignore all of those people. But those comments about wasted rent began to settle into my stomach. Each month I'd write the rent check and feel a little queasy. What if we were wasting our money? What if the kids were going to miss out if we didn't buy a house?

So, I started looking for a house, and I fell in love with a ninety-five-year-old home in a historic district. Then I talked my husband into the home. Even though there were giant red flags everywhere, from the electrical system to the lack of central air, I ignored those flashing warning signs and pushed ahead.

Over the past twenty years, we've paid the financial and emotional costs of dealing with a lovely historical home that came fully equipped with outdated everything. Yet God has used this home to shelter us, protect our children, and secure us during financial uncertainty. God has taken care of us in spite of our initial worry-driven actions.

Recall the situation you described above. What are some of the consequences you have faced because you acted wrongly—whether foolishly or sinfully—out of worry?

Now it is time for Joshua to question the Gibeonites about their deception. I imagine that he is struggling to hold his temper, like a parent trying to calmly question a teenager who has lied about coming in after curfew. It's in this questioning that an interesting conversation takes place.

Read Joshua 9:24-25 in the margin. What does Joshua learn from the Gibeonites about the reason for their deception?

24 They replied, "We did it because we—your servants—were clearly told that the LORD your God commanded his servant Moses to give you this entire land and to destroy all the people living in it. So we feared greatly for our lives because of you. That is why we have done this. 25 Now we are at your mercy—do to us whatever you think is right."

(Joshua 9:24-25)

Does the tone of their explanation sound familiar? The Gibeonites' story is similar to the words that we heard from Rahab the prostitute.

Review Joshua 2:9-13 and mark each statement T (true) or F (false) to indicate the similarities between the comments of Rahab and the Gibeonites:

_____ **1. Both proclaimed that God gave the Israelites the land of Canaan.**

_____ **2. Both believed that the kings would eventually overwhelm Joshua and the army.**

_____ **3. Both were terrified because of the Israelites' conquests.**

_____ **4. Both wanted to fight the Israelites in hopes of saving their lives.**

_____ **5. Both asked the Israelites for help in hopes of being saved from destruction.**

How amazing it must have been for Joshua and the leaders to hear about not one but two groups of people within the Promised Land who believed God without actually seeing Him at work. What a testimony that is to us today! It reminds us that even when we melt down, God doesn't give up on us; and we shouldn't give up trying to walk by faith. Holding on to faith is one way we can attack the roots of our worries.

Look at Joshua 9:24 again. What do the Gibeonites believe?

Even though they are deceptive, how do you see them express courage?

Now look again at verse 25. How does this verse show their ultimate willingness to act in obedience?

Although the Gibeonites do not enjoy a covenant relationship with God as the Israelites do, they believe in God anyway. They trust that if God has said He is going to give the Israelites the Promised Land, it will happen. Though we cannot condone their dishonesty, we can commend their faith.

Answers: 1. T 2. F 3. T 4. T 5. T

Here's one more piece of encouragement for us—whether we are seekers, new Christians, or longtime believers. Rahab and the Gibeonites remind us that we don't have to know everything in order to trust God's promises, have courage, and act in obedience. When we act out of trust and obedience, we attack the roots of our worries.

Read Psalm 112 below, and in the space provided, list some of the blessings that those who trust and obey will receive.

Praise the Lord!

How joyful are those who fear the Lord
and delight in obeying his commands.
² Their children will be successful everywhere;
an entire generation of godly people will be blessed.
³ They themselves will be wealthy,
and their good deeds will last forever.
⁴ Light shines in the darkness for the godly.
They are generous, compassionate, and righteous.
⁵ Good comes to those who lend money generously
and conduct their business fairly.
⁶ Such people will not be overcome by evil.
Those who are righteous will be long remembered.
⁷ They do not fear bad news;
they confidently trust the Lord to care for them.
⁸ They are confident and fearless
and can face their foes triumphantly.
⁹ They share freely and give generously to those in need.
Their good deeds will be remembered forever.
They will have influence and honor.
¹⁰ The wicked will see this and be infuriated.
They will grind their teeth in anger;
they will slink away, their hopes thwarted.

Blessings for those who trust and obey:

I love how this psalm begins with "Praise the Lord!" Honoring God with our words is another way we attack the roots of our worries. When I was a kid and heard people say "Praise the Lord!" in church, it felt cliché. People looked enthusiastic when they said it, but I didn't understand the story behind their

> **Loving like Christ is one of the most powerful ways we can attack the roots of our worries!**

Today's Takeaway

God can use a little bit of faith to overcome a lot of worry.

words. Yet as I've walked with God and have struggled through hard times while holding on to God, I have experienced the blessings that can come only from fearing God instead of living in fear.

Psalm 112 tells us the story behind "Praise the Lord!" We give thanks to God for how He blesses us and gives us joy even in the midst of all that we worry about and fear. I love verse 4: "Light shines in the darkness for the godly. / They are generous, compassionate, and righteous." There are a lot of things that I can be in life, but there are two things that I do not want to be: lost in the dark or afraid to love.

When we trust God, He guides our way in life. If you feel lost in your life and aren't sure which way to go, ask God to tell you. The Holy Spirit leads and guides us into truth so that we know which way to go, even when life is uncertain. When we know that God will show us the way, we stop fearing for our lives; and that gives us the strength to love others. We love through generosity and compassion as imitators of Christ. And loving like Christ is one of the most powerful ways we can attack the roots of our worries!

Reread Psalm 112:7 on page 125. What bad news are you trying to deal with right now?

How can you see God taking care of you in this situation?

What promises of God apply to what you are facing?

My friend, today is the day that God wants you to be freed from the influence of age-old worries in your life. You attack the root of your worries when you anchor yourself in your faith, respond to God in obedience, praise God for His work in your life, and then love others as Christ loves you. Similar to the way that the soldiers placed their feet across the necks of those kings, God wants you to find victory over worry!

Apply It: Wisdom Wednesday

"If you do catch yourself worrying even after you've done what was wise, remember that God is bigger than our problems, and that he wants us to hand them over to him. Worry then becomes a signal alerting us that it's time to pray."[4]

—Craig Groeschel

Prayer

Dear God, there are times when I get worried and I'm tempted to do the wrong thing. In those moments, remind me of the words of Psalm 112:7 that tell me I do not have to fear bad news and that I can be confident You will take care of me. In Jesus' name, Amen.

DAY 4: WHEN HURRY CAUSES WORRY

How much of our worry happens because we're in a hurry? Is it just me? Hurry is another root of worry.

I can't tell you how many times that I've frantically yelled, "I'm running out of time!" That has been my experience whether I was sneaking out of one meeting to rush to another or writing a blog post with one eye watching the clock tick past midnight. Time and worry go together like peanut butter and jelly. (I love a yummy word picture!)

Most of our worry is tied to the idea that we'll run out of time before we can get to our preferred solution or happy ending.

We worry that we won't have the money in time.

We worry that the other person won't stay in the relationship long enough.

We worry that the medicine won't work in time.

We worry that there's not enough time with our kids.

Ever since the beginning of the world, we've worried about the limits of time. But in God's economy, time is a tool, not a limit. It's not possible for us to turn back, pause, or advance time, but for God all time-related things are possible because God exists outside of time. Today we're going to watch one of those impossibilities take place.

On Monday, we began reading about the alliances of the kings who came together in order to fight the Israelites. Remember, it was a whole lot of kings! Now those kings realize that the Gibeonites have struck a treaty with the Israelites, which means that this alliance threatens the other kings in Canaan.

Read Joshua 10:5. What do the kings do?

As you recall, Gibeon is a large, important city; and the alliance of kings does not want Joshua and the Israelites to have access to Gibeon's resources and potential. Not only that, but this alliance of kings is likely angry that Gibeon, probably a former ally, has now taken sides with the newest, biggest threat in their land.

The Canaanite kings plan their attack. Luckily, the Gibeonites aren't in the fight alone.

Read Joshua 10:6-9. How many men does Joshua take with him?

What is God's message to Joshua before he goes to fight?

How long do Joshua and the army march?

Not only do the Israelites honor their agreement by not killing the Gibeonites, but they also fight to protect them. Rather than treating them with the "we'll get there when we can" approach, Joshua and all of his army double-time their way to the rescue.

Read Joshua 10:10-11. What two things does God do to help the Israelite army?

What causes more deaths: hailstones or swords?

My first job out of college was adjusting insurance claims. Hailstorm claims always fascinated me because the hail would shoot from the sky at a damaging velocity only to evaporate upon impact. It didn't even stick around to take responsibility for the mess!

Here in Joshua 10 we read about a killer hailstorm, literally. In fact, we're told that more of the Israelites' enemies are killed by the hailstorm than by the sword. If you're an Amorite soldier and you survive the hailstorm and battle, you've got quite a story to tell the folks back home.

But God's not done demonstrating His power on behalf of the Israelites. Now Joshua steps up in a bold way.

Read Joshua 10:12-13. What does Joshua ask God to do?

What happens, and how long does it last?

On the day the Lord gives the Israelites victory over the Amorites, Joshua prays to the Lord in front of all the people of Israel, saying, "Let the sun stand still over Gibeon, / and the moon over the valley of Aijalon" (Joshua 10:12). We read that as a result of Joshua's prayer, the sun stands still for a whole day. In other words, it does not set for twenty-four hours.

In Joshua's time, military engagement ended when the sun went down. There were no night vision goggles. Like my childhood summer baseball games, everyone picked up their toys and went home when the sun went down.

Now, this longest-day account is hotly debated by scientists and skeptics. Some scientists dispute the biblical account even though there are independent reports of a long day.[5] Others suggest a few possible explanations:

- **Possibility #1:** The earth stopped rotating. Natural laws would have been thrown into chaos, but God could have managed those as well.
- **Possibility #2:** The miracle of refraction. The earth continued to rotate, but God created a mirage so that it appeared that the sun was still out.
- **Possibility #3**: The earth slowed but didn't stop. God slowed the rotation to last an additional day.[6]

These are just a few possibilities. I want to encourage you to research this for yourself. In fact, good students of the Bible ask questions and dig into the text in order to discover its meaning and application.

I find it interesting that although it is Joshua who calls on God for this miracle, the effects of the miracle would be seen around the world. As Joshua and the fighting men are conquering the Amorite kings, the stationary sun in the sky is testifying to the rest of the world of God's glory and power. I wonder what our imagined Israelite sister thought about the sun standing still? Would she look to the extended sunlight and acknowledge it is likely a miracle of God, or would she keep her head down and run from one chore to the next? God is always performing miracles around us, friend. Let's make sure to keep our heads up and slow down so we can catch a glimpse of the miraculous in our everyday lives.

Like Joshua, you and I have times in our lives when we're fighting to defeat certain challenges and wonder if we'll be able to hang in there until the end.

But we can find encouragement in the takeaway lesson from this story: when we're accomplishing God's purposes for our lives, God runs the time clock.

Do you feel any pressure or worry when you think about your current schedule or the time line of a certain challenge? What do you worry about neglecting or not finishing?

How fast do you feel that your life is moving right now? Circle a number on the scale below:

Relaxed				Somewhat stressed				Frantic	
1	2	3	4	5	6	7	8	9	10

If you had asked me that question three years ago, I would have answered 10+! My life only had one speed: Go faster! I moved from one place to the next without any margin in between. My brand of hurry meant late arrivals, fast-talking, and a bad habit of interrupting. My "hurry" had me going through drive-thrus, eating in my car, and rushing moments with my kids between meetings and practices.

According to the dictionary, the word *hurry* means "to move or act with speed or haste…rush."[7] That describes that period of my life perfectly. When I look back on those hurried years, I recall a forgetful memory, a racing heartbeat, a shortened temper, and an unsatisfied heart. Perhaps this is why Joshua's bold prayer means so much to me, because I know that if I was out there on the battlefield and the sun was going down, I might have started to worry and take my eyes off the fight in front of me.

When we hurry, it's often because there's more on our plate than God intends for us. In *The Best Yes*, Lysa TerKeurst offers this insight into how hurry happens in many of our lives: "Other people's requests dictate the decisions that we make. We become slaves to others' demands when we let our time become dictated by requests. We will live reactive lives instead of proactive."[8] Can you relate?

How much of your "hurry" is because of your personal schedule and/or the requests and demands of others? Circle one response:

None	Some	Most	All

What makes Joshua's prayer so powerful is that even though he was running out of time to win the battle, he knew that he was doing exactly what God had called him to do. That's the confidence that Joshua had when he prayed that prayer!

When I'm thinking about my God-given roles in life as a wife, mother, daughter, sister, friend, speaker, and author, I can have confidence that God will provide the time I need to care for that which He has called me to do. But it is my responsibility to protect the time that God has given me.

As you reflect on your daily schedule, can you identify any time stealers that take unnecessary time away from your key responsibilities? List any below:

Let's go back to Joshua's prayer. Can you imagine praying and asking God for something so bold? Joshua's request for the sun to stand still gives us some important insight into him as a man of faith. Joshua knew God's vision for his life and purposed to live out that mission. He didn't ask God to make the sun stand still just so that he could defeat the enemy; he asked God to do the impossible because God is the One who sent Joshua on the mission in the first place.

What can we learn from Joshua's prayer? In his book *Sun Stand Still*, Steven Furtick describes Joshua's kind of faith as audacious, which is bold or daring. Then he challenges us with a question: "Does the brand of faith you live by produce the kinds of results in your life that you read about in the biblical stories or men and women of faith?"[9]

If you want to model Joshua's audacious faith, Furtick outlines these five steps to take when praying a "sun stand still" prayer:

1. Activate your audacious faith.
2. Approach God with boldness.
3. Ask specifically for what is humanly impossible.
4. Advance toward the answer.
5. Give God all the glory.[10]

Joshua did all of these things. And as one who battles worry, I want to be like Joshua. After all of the times that God told Joshua to be strong and courageous as well as not to be afraid or discouraged, here in this bold prayer Joshua's heartbeat thumps in rhythm with God's purpose for his life. I want my heart to beat in rhythm with God's purpose because it's then that I'm most likely to be inspired to pray a "sun stand still" prayer like Joshua. What about you?

What is something that seems impossible unless God steps in and empowers you to do it? Name it below:

Jesus looked at them intently and said, "Humanly speaking, it is impossible. But with God everything is possible."

(Matthew 19:26)

But when you ask him, be sure that your faith is in God alone. Do not waver, for a person with divided loyalty is as unsettled as a wave of the sea that is blown and tossed by the wind.

(James 1:6)

Read Matthew 19:26 in the margin. What does this verse say about our ability versus God's ability?

Now read James 1:6 in the margin. What should we remember when we come before God?

When we read about God making the sun stand still or sending hailstones from heaven, it's easy to dismiss the possibility that God won't show that kind of power in our lives. Yet if you've ever witnessed what happens when you pray for someone far from God and then He begins to change the person into an on-fire believer, then you've seen that kind of power. A transformed human life is just as powerful as the sun standing still for a day. And if you've been praying that kind of prayer but are still waiting to see change, remember other times and ways God has answered prayer and shown His faithfulness, and continue to persist in prayer.

As a longtime former church staffer, we'd encourage people to invite their friends to church. So often people would commit to pray for a family member or friend but would tell us, "Oh, so-and-so will never come to church." We'd say, "Invite them anyway. You never know what God can do." One of those never-come-to-church couples were Kim and Clark. Someone invited them without much expectation that the couple would show up. But they did! They kept showing up and eventually gave their lives to Christ. For many, many years, I've watched them grow and serve in some of the most incredible ways.

Sister, God is still answering "sun stand still" prayers! The question that you must ask is this: Am I willing to pray one?

Write your own "sun stand still" prayer to God about something in your life that is impossible without God.

How easy or difficult was it for you to write that prayer? It's far easier for us to let hurry lead us to worry, imagining the worst of the worst rather than dreaming of God's ability to do the impossible. At the time that I'm writing this to you, I'm focused on a consistent and persistent sun-stand-still prayer in my own life. I don't have the power to do what needs to get done, but I believe that in God, all things are possible. I'm going to keep praying that impossible prayer, and I'm going to have faith that God will answer that prayer In His time and in the very best way.

Apply It: Temperature Check Thursday

Today it's time for your weekly check to think about the progress you're making. How are you doing? Take a moment to honestly assess where you are in your worry battle.

Circle the number that indicates where you are today:

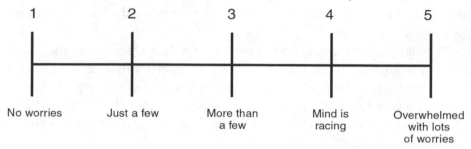

1	2	3	4	5
No worries	Just a few	More than a few	Mind is racing	Overwhelmed with lots of worries

If you circled a 1 or 2, what tools and insights that you've implemented so far are helping you to keep worry on a low level?

What promises have been most helpful for you to remember?

If you circled a 3, 4, or 5, why do you think you're struggling?

Prayer

God, You make all things possible! Thank You for reminding me of that today. I will no longer let hurry drive me into worry. Instead, I will remember that You will give me enough time to do all that You've called me to do. As I trust You to answer my "sun stand still" prayer, I will wait in faith that You will answer according to Your perfect will and in Your perfect timing. Amen.

Extra Insight

"If you really believe what God has said about His unlimited ability, then guess what?—you may have prayed your last safe, undersized prayer for the rest of your life, both for yourself and for others."

—Priscilla Shirer[11]

Today's Takeaway

When we're accomplishing God's purposes for our lives, God runs the time clock.

On the Map

To find the approximate location of Makkedah on the map (page 11), draw a line between Jerusalem and Lachish; then draw a circle halfway between the two cities.

DAY 5: STANDING ON THE NECK OF WORRY

I love all kinds of board games, including checkers. In the game of checkers, only the smartest, savviest players know how to advance all of their pieces or "soldiers" across the board, jumping over and capturing the opposition's soldiers. I must admit that savvy player is usually someone other than me! I rarely see that big move. Yet when I do manage to get a soldier to the other side of the board, it's a magnificent moment. The sweetest words you can say during the game are "King me!"

The more often a player says "King me," the less chance the other player has to win. When a soldier becomes a king, so much more becomes possible! Kings travel across the board farther and faster than the ordinary soldiers. On a single move, a king can capture multiple soldiers with multiple jumps. Yet for all of the additional moving power, the wise player always remembers that an ordinary soldier can still capture a king.

This week we've been looking at how to attack the roots of our worries so that, ultimately, we can defeat the kings of worry. Today in Joshua 10, we will learn from the army of Israelite soldiers as it captures and defeats a great horde of kings.

After defeating the Amorite kings, Joshua and the fighting men return to the Israelite camp at Gilgal. But they don't have much time to rest because Joshua gets some intel that those Amorite kings have fled from the fighting and are still sticking together.

Read Joshua 10:16-19, and answer the following questions.

Who is hiding in the cave at Makkedah?

Joshua gives two instructions regarding the discovery of the kings and one regarding the enemy:

Order #1: Put _____ **at the mouth of the cave.**

Order #2: Post men to _____ **it.**

Order #3: Keep _____ **the enemy.**

Even as Joshua instructs the men to contain the kings, he doesn't lose sight of the assignment to conquer their enemies

Read Joshua 10:20-21. What is the outcome of the Israelites' fighting?

Again the Israelite army is victorious over their enemies. However, this time a few survivors manage to make it back to their hometowns. Can you imagine those surviving enemy soldiers giving a firsthand account of what they saw and experienced during battle after returning home? Of course, when their friends and families tell that they saw the sun stand still while they were away, the soldiers can testify to that as well—and it's some story!

Joshua and the soldiers are now camped at Makkedah, and it is time to deal with the Amorite kings trapped in the cave.

Read Joshua 10:22-24. What does Joshua command the men of Israel and the army commanders to do?

It's not clear if all of the men participated in this or only a representative number. Yet for every man who placed his foot on the neck of an Amorite king, it must have been a strange yet triumphant feeling to literally stand victoriously over their enemies.

Joshua could have commanded the men to put their feet on the necks of random soldiers, and that would have been powerful. Yet humbling a king in this way was like putting an exclamation point at the end of a victory. Those Amorite kings once had sat on thrones with power and influence, but now they were humiliated by having the dirty, stinky, dusty feet of their enemies pressed upon their necks. They once had influence over cites and vast armies, but now they are laid low. They are a symbol for the long-standing roots of worry in our lives—perhaps even since childhood.

What are some long-standing worries that have influenced your life and the decisions you've made?

Extra Insight

"To influence others you have to help move them to new realities and possibilities. You can't take them where you haven't led yourself. You must be willing to confront your fears and lead others through theirs."[12]

—Jenni Catron

As you fight for victory over fear and worry, you will provide an attractive model for others to follow.

How have you struggled to fight your worry battle because of the power and influence of those long-standing worries?

Now Joshua addresses the men with familiar words that we've heard before.

Write Joshua 10:25 in the space below:

Do you want to know what I love about Joshua 10:25? It's that Joshua is the one speaking these words. He has heard them over and over again from God, and now he stands in front of his men as their God-ordained leader, repeating the same words. His words aren't for that moment only; they are to be burned into their memories forever. They are the prophetic words of victory spoken man to men. As the men stand with their feet on the necks of the kings and Joshua calls them to abandon fear, this moment demonstrates just how much Joshua has grown as a leader.

Like Joshua, your level of fear or worry will transmit to those who look up to you or depend on you. Conversely, as you fight for victory over fear and worry, you will provide an attractive model for others to follow. Even while fighting the battle, your example will speak volumes as you keep your mind focused on truth.

Read each Scripture and identify the reason we don't need to be afraid:

Genesis 15:1—Do not be afraid for _____

Isaiah 40:9-10—Do not be afraid for _____

No one is exempt from needing to be reminded of these truths. Leadership author and coach Jenni Catron recalls facing a season in her own life when she was filled with tremendous insecurities about her job. Fears and worries bounced around her mind and "what if" questions kept her up at night. Thankfully, she gave voice to all of the deep, dark, and ugly feelings with her husband, and he was able to speak truth to her.

It doesn't matter if you are a leadership coach like Jenni, a line worker in a factory, a business professional, a college student with a tough course load, or a stay-at-home mom, don't beat yourself up for having fears. Rather, focus your efforts on the reasons why you don't need to be afraid.

Read 2 Timothy 1:7 in the margin. According to this verse, what has God not given us, and what *has* He given us?

For God has not given us a spirit of fear and timidity, but of power, love, and self-discipline.

(2 Timothy 1:7)

Fear does not come from God. It might come from within us, but it does not come from God.

In the battles that follow, Joshua and the Israelites move from town to town capturing each city, eliminating the people, and killing the king. As we read the remainder of chapter 10, you might be wondering why God orders the Israelites to kill everyone, including innocent men, women, and children. I have struggled with this as well, because it doesn't seem fair.

Here are some insights that can give you something to think about, as well as provide direction for your own self-study. God was establishing a nation as He promised, which meant that battles would need to occur for the occupation of the land. Earlier this week, we learned of Canaan's curse and the prophecy against the people of Canaan, as well as God's proclamation to Abraham about the Promised Land (Genesis 12:1-3; 15:16). Though God gave the Israelites the Promised Land, the current inhabitants weren't going to just hand it over to them. This meant there would be bloodshed. You might say that war came with the territory. God was establishing not only a people but a nation that would be set apart and, ultimately, would be a blessing to the whole world. As author and pastor David Kalas points out:

> The New Tesatment seems comparatively free of such carnage, but then the New Testament also covers a fraction of the time that Old Testament history represents. It was written during a time of relative peace under the unified Roman Empire. And, most significantly, the church at this time is not a nation with borders and battles, but an international body that endeavors to cross all borders.[13]

It's time for the Israelites to confront an even bigger wave of opposition.

Read Joshua 11:1-5. How is the size of the combined army described in verse 4?

As we learned earlier, King Jabin of Hazor is the king over all of the other kings, who rule over individual city-state territories with their own infrastructures and cultures. Those kings report to the king in Hazor, and he is subject to the pharaoh in Egypt.

Now, I'm not one for big-budget ancient war movies like 300 or *Gladiator*, but I've seen clips of those epic battles. And it seems to me like the scenario described in verses 1-5 is lifted out of one of those movies. The kings combined their armies and resources into a huge army described as numerous as the sand on the seashore!

Envision your favorite beach. Now, picture soldiers, horses, and chariots packed onto the beach as far as the eye can see. Their presence would create quite an intimidating scene!

Now, imagine that you're Joshua. You've seen God do some mighty things, but the sight of this great army must be just a little unsettling, right? No doubt this was true for Joshua, because it's here that God speaks to him some familiar words.

Read Joshua 11:6. What does God tell Joshua?

Fighting an army of this size will require a substantial amount of courage and faith, and so God tells Joshua not to be afraid because He will bring them victory. The Israelite army had to know and believe that God would be on its side so that even as the soldiers grew fatigued they would know that quitting wasn't an option. As wave after wave of enemy soldiers would test their resolve and endurance, they would be able to press on remembering that the Lord was with them.

Even as Joshua is surely acknowledging the reality of the coming battle, he doesn't stall or shy away.

Read Joshua 11:7. What do Joshua and the whole army do?

If we don't get the jump on worry, it's going to get the jump on us.

Joshua and his men go to fight the battle that needs to be won, and the Scriptures say that they attack suddenly.

When worry is threatening, we can know that if we don't get the jump on worry, it's going to get the jump on us. The best thing to do when we're facing a battle is to go out and fight in faith before worry even has a chance to begin.

Reread Joshua 11:6 and then read Joshua 11:9. What did God instruct Joshua to do to the horses and chariots?

If you're an animal lover, it might be hard to understand why God would order them to cut the hamstrings of the enemy's horses. Scholars explain that if Joshua and the Israelite army, who have only swords as weapons, were to take the chariots and horses of the kings, then they might begin to attribute their future victories to their prowess rather than to God's power. God has promised to give them the land, and He wants them to see that He keeps His promises—not only because He wants to give them the land, but also so that future generations can hear the stories of God's miraculous and powerful works.

There are times in life when we don't feel equipped to deal with the problems we're facing. That's why we worry, right? Yet in those times when we feel ill-equipped and we elevate our prayers to the God who is fully able, we get to witness God's power and provision on our behalf. And when we tell the story of victory, God is the main character who receives the glory—rather than us siphoning off some of the praise for ourselves.

Read Zechariah 4:6 in the margin. Can you think of a time when you were the underdog in a situation but God's Spirit helped you come out on top? If so, describe it below:

"It is not by force nor by strength, but by my Spirit, says the L ORD of Heaven's Armies."

(Zechariah 4:6)

This week's study strikes close to our hearts, from putting our feet across the necks of longtime worries to dealing with the tricky issue of secondhand worry. Whatever issue is pressing on your life right now, your victory over it depends on fighting in faith, remembering that God is with you and for you in every circumstance. Even if you've failed to beat those worries in the past or those worries have come back, don't beat yourself up! Put your fighting friends into action, applying the tools that you've learned, and before long you'll begin to experience God's victory over worry!

Apply It: Freedom Friday

Is there a victory that you've experienced this week in your battle over worry? Remember, a victory over worry can be anything, including:

- repeating a promise of God to interrupt negative thinking;
- using a tool that you've learned; or
- practicing a spiritual discipline such as meditation, fasting, or prayer, and then experiencing a connection with God that drew you close to Him.

Today's Takeaway

Fighting against worry isn't for the faint of heart. I've got to want God's victory and not give up until I receive it.

Describe your victory this week:

Prayer

Dear God, the imagery of Joshua and the soldiers standing with their feet on the necks of the mighty kings is a powerful picture of how I can put my feet on the neck of worry. I will not be afraid because You are with me everywhere I go. Show me where I am putting my faith in my abilities, and remind me to place 100 percent of my faith in You. In Jesus' name, Amen.

Joshua 9:14—The Israelites did not consult God

Joshua 10:8-10—God gave the victory

Joshua 10:12—Joshua's sun-stand-still prayer

We've got to know our _____.

And then…we've got to stay and _____ for the right ones.

God is the God of the _____.

Mark 10:27—"Everything is possible with God."

1 Corinthians 15:57—Resurrection power

Ephesians 2:4—God is rich in mercy

Time is a _____ for us, but it is just a _____ for God.

Worry is when you're _____ but you're not doing anything productive.

Concern is when there are _____ _____ that you can take to support and encourage without controlling.

See page 206 for answers.

CLAIMING OUR INHERITANCE

Receiving Our Victory

Joshua 12–18

MEMORY VERSE

"For my part, I wholeheartedly followed the LORD my God."
(Joshua 14:8b)

Here we are at the halfway point in the Book of Joshua! The first eleven chapters have been about preparing for battle and then fighting to claim the Promised Land. The fighting men have been at war for a long time. Now the fighting is winding down, and the Israelites are preparing to claim their inheritance.

Chapter 11, which we covered last week, and chapter 12, which begins our study this week, are both reflective chapters on the battles that are fought before and after the Israelites enter the Promised Land. We will begin our week of study reflecting on the Israelites' battles, as well as our own.

In the military, there is a term for post-battle analysis called AAR, or after-action review. This is an honest appraisal of performance and a tool to correct shortcomings. As we work through this week's study, we'll reflect on how God positions the Israelites for victory. We'll also see some of the ways the Israelites do not follow God's directives to completion. Though they killed the kings, we'll discover that they do not completely claim their victory.

This week also provides an opportunity for you to complete your own personal AAR. We've been waging war against worry for four weeks, and this is a good time to reflect on what God has been doing in your life. So, let's get started!

DAY 1: TAG-TEAM VICTORY

If you've ever watched big-time wrestling like WWE, you know that there's a popular team event called "tag-team" wrestling. This is where two-person teams compete with one person from each team in the ring at a time. Then, if there is fatigue, injury, or near defeat, the competitor can "tag" his or her teammate and allow the teammate to take over the fight.

In a sense, Joshua 12 is a recap of the tag-team effort between Moses and Joshua. While Moses died many years before, this chapter provides a summary of all the battles fought by Moses, Joshua, and the Israelites.

Read Joshua 12:2-6. What were the names of the two kings that Moses defeated east of the Jordan River?

King Og actually ruled over two kingdoms. Where were the royal residencies of those kingdoms located? (v. 4)

If you remember from earlier in our study, King Og was a descendant of the Rephaites, a race of giant people. After King Sihon and King Og were defeated, their land was assigned to the Israelite tribes of Reuben, Gad, and the half-tribe of Manasseh, who decided to settle east of the Jordan River.

The rest of Joshua 12 catalogues the kings living west of the Jordan River who were defeated. Before we study this part, check out the last sentence in the chapter.

Read Joshua 12:24b. How many kings were defeated?

That's a lot of kings! Joshua 12:9-24 catalogues the entire list of defeated kings and their kingdoms of the west. I wonder if Joshua knew in advance that he'd be fighting thirty-one kings and their armies. The thought of fighting just one king seems daunting to me! Imagine when Joshua and his men dragged their weary bodies back to camp after each victory. They'd eat some food and collapse into sleep only to wake up the next morning to begin training and planning for their next attack.

As you reflect on your life, what is harder for you to endure: occasional major worries or persistent minor worries? Why?

35 Can anything ever separate us from Christ's love? Does it mean he no longer loves us if we have trouble or calamity, or are persecuted, or hungry, or destitute, or in danger, or threatened with death?… 37 No, despite all these things, overwhelming victory is ours through Christ, who loved us.

(Romans 8:35, 37)

Read Romans 8:35 in the margin. List the struggles that have been a part of your life:

Now read verse 37. What kind of victory are we promised in spite of these struggles?

Take a moment and sit with this powerful truth. In the New Living Translation, verse 37 describes our victory as overwhelming. I love this because God isn't promising us a razor-thin margin of victory at the finish line but a "you can't touch this" victory that leaves the enemy of our souls crushed in the dust. Amen!

Do you ever think there was a day when Joshua opened his eyes and said, "God, do I have to go out and fight again today? Can't we just take the day off?"

Because he was a man of mission, I'm not sure Joshua actually whined about the years of battle, but I am sure he might have been weary at times.

How are you doing today when it comes to your worry battle? Are you energized, feeling battle weary, or close to giving up?

There are times when I just want God to kick my worry in the teeth and make it go away once and for all. But then I remember that when I battle worry, it causes me to worship my worry right out the door. Fighting worry requires my constant submission to God's way of life, the choice to be obedient to God, and a commitment to the tools and disciplines that help win the fight. And just because I've gotten in position and experienced God's power over worry in one area does not mean that victory applies to other areas. I know I have to reposition myself for other worry battles, too.

You may know some of the more popular Scriptures that deal with worry. But whether or not you're familiar with these verses, I pray they encourage your heart today.

Read the following verses and summarize the message of each:

Psalm 56:11

Proverbs 3:24

Isaiah 41:13

1 Peter 5:7

The writer of Psalm 118, who is unnamed, calls us to celebrate God's faithfulness by remembering what He has done. Though scholars debate whether this psalm speaks of Israel in a personified sense or is about David or another king of Israel, many of the verses remind me of Joshua.

Read Psalm 118:10-13. What are some similar battle experiences shared by the writer or subject of the psalm and Joshua?

Here are a few observations. Both the writer and Joshua faced hostile nations that surrounded and attacked them (vv. 10-11). While the writer compares the

enemy soldiers to bees, the great horde of kings Joshua faced were as numerous as sand (v. 12). Both the writer and Joshua faced enemies that did their best to kill them (v. 13).

Now read verse 14, and write it below:

When we get ourselves in position, God delivers our victory.

As we see in Exodus 15:2, this verse originated with Moses after the Israelites crossed the Red Sea and escaped Pharaoh's army. Moses and the Israelites sang this song of deliverance in worship of a mighty God who, in the words of the wise preachers from my childhood church, "is a God who makes a way out of no way."

Why did both Moses and the psalm writer say that God was their "strength and song"? What does that mean?

The Hebrew word for "strength" is *oz*,[1] a derivative of the root word *azaz*,[2] which means "prevail." To say that God is our strength is to say that God will prevail. Claiming that God is our strength reinforces the fighting-in-faith principle that when we get ourselves in position, God delivers our victory.

When it comes to God and music, God loves to sing! Since God is perfect, we know that He always sings in perfect pitch. And I'm sure He claps on beat, too!

For the LORD your God is living among you.
He is a mighty savior.
He will take delight in you with gladness.
With his love, he will calm all your fears.
He will rejoice over you with joyful songs.
(Zephaniah 3:17)

Read Zephaniah 3:17 in the margin. What kind of songs does God sing—and where does He sing them?

There are more than four hundred references to singing in the Bible, as well as dozens of direct commandments to sing. And of course, there's the Book of Psalms, which is a collection of songs. God sings, and He wants us to sing, too. There are a few good reasons why we should sing, especially when we're in the midst of battling worry. But the big takeaway is that when we sing to God, the music ministers deep within our souls to uplift and encourage us.

One final word: Sometimes belting out just one or two uplifting worship songs can short-circuit a brewing panic or meltdown. You don't even have to sing on key! It may not work in every case, but I've found that when I sing out to God during a moment of panic, He reminds me of His promises of peace. Singing or listening to worship songs helps my fighting friends disconnect WorryFlix and fire-up FaithFlix in my heart and mind. Give it a try!

Apply It: Monday Motivation

Do you need a pick-me-up today? Music is motivating! Gift yourself with 10–15 minutes of your favorite worship music—either now or some other time of your day. Choose songs that remind you that God has been with you, has stood beside you, and has made you victorious in your battle with worry.

If you're not sure where to find worship music, just search "worship music" on YouTube or any other music streaming service.

Prayer

Dear God, I love that You promise me overwhelming victory, even though my life might feel overwhelmed at times. Even when I'm tired and weary, You stand beside me, calming my fears. Just as You sing over me, I want to sing songs that give praise to You. Thank You, God, for being so good and faithful to me. Amen.

DAY 2: A LITTLE BIT OF WORRY IS STILL WORRY

Yesterday we learned that Joshua and the Israelites defeated thirty-one kings. Today we're going to look at a few of those defeated kingdoms, including some clues about the kingdoms based on the meanings of their names, before we learn a valuable lesson as we move toward victory in our own battle. Though each of those kingdoms lost their king in battle, the Israelites did not completely drive out the people as God commanded; and we will see that the failure to follow through on God's orders would hold tremendous consequences for His people in time. The same is true for us when we do not do all we can to drive out worry completely.

Last week we looked at two insights that can help to shed light on why God might have called for the complete destruction of the Canaanites, Amorites, and their neighbors. Now, we're going to explore a third.

Read Numbers 33:55-56. What were the Israelites supposed to do, and why?

What type of painful symbol would the people living in the land become to the Israelites?

Fighting in faith is not easy, but it gets easier each day when I practice submission, commitment, and discipline.

What ominous warning does God give about what will happen if they are disobedient?

God paints a powerful word picture for how painful it will be for the Israelites to allow even a small number of the original inhabitants to remain in the Promised Land. Most of us are used to splinters in our hands, but God says that if the people are not removed, they will be like splinters in the Israelites' eyes.

When's the last time you had a splinter? There are no good splinters—ever. Isn't it amazing how something so small can cause so much pain. Once you have a splinter, the only thing on your mind is getting rid of it.

What could happen if you were to get a splinter in your eye?

God blesses those whose hearts are pure,

    for they will see God.

        (Matthew 5:8)

Extra Insight

The Greek word for "pure" is *katharos*, meaning purged and free from contaminating influences of sin.[3] The word "see" is *horaó*, and it means to properly perceive with the mind.[4]

Quite simply, you couldn't see. If you left the splinter in your eye, eventually the eye tissue would get infected, and you might even lose your sight.

God wanted the Israelites to remove the inhabitants from the land so that they would maintain their spiritual sight. If the Israelites lived among a small remnant of people who rejected God, eventually that small population would infect them and prevent them from seeing God. God prophesied that once the Israelites became blind to His presence in their lives, they would suffer through all sorts of difficulties and destruction.

We've acknowledged that at different times throughout our lifetimes, we will have skirmishes with worry about different things. But when we think about our current worry battle, our goal always should be to eliminate 100 percent of the worry about the particular situation or concern. We can't harbor a little fretting here or there because a little bit of worry is still worry. Likewise, a little bit of worry will eventually grow into a giant panic and meltdown.

This Old Testament example of the Israelites failing to drive out all of their enemies provides rich symbolism for us today in regard to how permissive we should be toward what God clearly calls us to avoid.

Read Matthew 5:8 in the margin. Underline the words *pure* and *see*. Then read the Extra Insight. With these definitions in mind, what is the meaning of this verse?

Do you think it is possible to keep a pure heart if we allow even the smallest splinters of worry to remain in place? Explain your response.

Read Joshua 12:9-24, which is a list of the thirty-one kings that Joshua and the Israelites defeated in order of their conquest. List below any names of cities that are familiar to you:

If you're anything like me, your list is short! Whenever I read the Old Testament, I'm challenged with the unfamiliar names and places, many of which I don't know how to pronounce. So I appreciate information that helps bring these details to life for me. In his devotional 31 *Keys to Possessing Your Promise*, Rodney Burton lists the thirty-one kingdoms and the interesting meanings behind the names of those kingdoms:[5]

1. Jericho—"city of the moon"
2. Ai—"a heap of ruins"
3. Jerusalem—"teaching of peace"
4. Hebron—"joining or association"
5. Jarmuth—"heights"
6. Lachish—"invincible"
7. Eglon—"calf-like"
8. Gezer—"a portion or piece"
9. Debir—"sanctuary
10. Geder—"wall or fence"
11. Hormah—"devoting"
12. Arad—"wild donkey"
13. Libnah—"transparency"
14. Abdullam—"justice of the people"
15. Makkedah—"place of the shepherd"
16. Bethel—"house of God"
17. Tappuah—"apple city"
18. Hepher—"a well"—going deeper
19. Aphek—"fortress"
20. Lasharon—"a plain" (rose of Sharon)
21. Madon—"strife"
22. Hazor—"castle"
23. Shimron-meron—"watch-height"
24. Achshaph—"I shall be bewitched"
25. Taanach—"sandy"
26. Megiddo—"place of the crowds"
27. Kedesh—"holy place"
28. Jokneam—"the people lament"
29. Dor—"generation"
30. Gilgal—"rolling away"
31. Tirzah—"favorable"

Based on these meanings, do any insights or assumptions jump out at you about any of the kingdoms? (There are no right or wrong answers here.)

Also based on these meanings, where would *you* want to live?

Besides the pronunciations of the names of these kingdoms, I'm challenged by their locations. If I'm honest, I also must deal with the niggling question: Why should I even care about these kingdoms? Well, there's actually good reason. So we're going to skip ahead and look at what happens years into the future after the Israelites are given their inheritance. Next week we will look at the inheritance process itself, but for now there is an important lesson for us to learn about what happens when we neglect to fully embrace and empower ourselves with God's victory. And we'll learn a little Bible geography along the way. Are you ready?

Put a placeholder at page 11, where we'll be turning to consult the map of Canaan.

1. Locate Gezer on the map. In which territory is the city of Gezer located? (*Clue*: Look in the western middle section of the Promised Land.)

Read Judges 1:27-29. Who did the Israelites (tribes of Manasseh and Ephraim) fail to drive out? What happened instead?

Judges 1 serves as a "where are they now?" update to the Israelites' attempt to occupy the land. Unfortunately, Gezer is just an example of one city where the Israelites failed to drive the Canaanite inhabitants from the land.

2. Locate Jerusalem on the map. In which territory is the city of Jerusalem located? (*Clue*: Look in the lower middle section of the Promised Land.)

Read Judges 1:21. Who did the Israelites (tribe of Benjamin) fail to drive out? What happened instead?

3. Find the following cities: Taanach, Dor, and Megiddo. They are all close together in the western middle section of the Promised Land. In which territory are they located?

Reread Judges 1:27-28. Why did the Israelites fail to drive out the Canaanites from the places listed above as well as a few other places? What happened once the Israelites grew stronger?

If you're like me, you might be wondering, "Wait a minute! If God promised to give the Israelites victory over their enemies, then why didn't the Israelites experience that victory?" But here's the question we should consider: Did God fail to keep His promise, or did the Israelites not follow through in faith on God's promise?

The answer to this question is repeated within the text numerous times. In fact, it jumped out from the page as I read. In my Bible translation, the phrase "did not drive out" is given multiple times as the primary reason the Israelites did not experience God's total victory. God promised them victory and empowered them for victory, but they failed to persevere and do their part.

The next logical question is why?

As I've studied Joshua and the Israelites, I've developed a kinship with these people who made the same kind of mistakes and missteps I'm making today. This imperfect band of people bless me because their story has been given to us by God in Scripture so that we may learn from them. So, as we explore why they did not drive out the Canaanites completely as God had commanded, let's approach this discussion with open hearts and minds so that we might benefit from their experience.

A few different scenarios might have kept the Israelites from driving out the Canaanites completely. I call these the four "worry drivers" because when we experience them, they will always drive us back to worry:

1. The Israelites got tired of fighting.
   (Weariness)
2. The Israelites grew an affinity for the inhabitants.
   (Compromise)
3. The Israelites stopped caring and decided to settle.
   (Apathy)
4. The Israelites lost faith that they could win.
   (Doubt)

Whenever I find myself wallowing in worry again after experiencing victory over a particular worry, I know I'm dealing with one or more of these worry drivers. In fact, while writing this Bible study, I found myself battling a particular worry that God has given me victory over in the past. He has been so faithful, yet last week I realized that some old WorryFlix episodes were playing regularly in my mind about this concern. Worse yet, I didn't care to stop them because I'd experienced these worries before and didn't want to deal with them in that moment, which sounds a lot like apathy. Even though those worries upset me, I just let them keep playing in my mind. Can you relate? Is there an active worry driver in your life that you are ignoring because you don't want to deal with it?

Do you sense that you're failing to experience God's victory in any area in your life? If so, check the worry driver(s) that might be getting in your way:

_____ **Weariness**　　　　_____ **Compromise**

_____ **Apathy**　　　　_____ **Doubt**

If we think back to the Israelites' victories at Jericho and Ai, we see no evidence of these worry drivers. In fact, we see their opposites—our fighting friends Peace, Courage, and Strength. As we've learned, these are the friends who can help us fight in faith whenever weariness, compromise, apathy, or doubt try to drive us back to worry. Thankfully, I was able to enlist the help of these fighting friends to push back the worry driver of apathy and gain victory over this recurring worry once again. Though I entertained the worry for a period, I was unwilling to return to the endless cycle of worry. Once we experience God's victory over worry, we are unsatisfied with going back to that kind of captivity. We must acknowledge that even a little bit of worry is still worry and erosive to our freedom. As we've said previously, there will be times when worry will bust through the door of our hearts and minds, but we always have immediate access to the power to drive worry right back out!

Philippians 4:6-7 provides the best recalibration for getting back into fighting position. It's one of the most popular verses on not worrying in the Bible. Write it below in your own words:

What does God want you to know today as you reflect on these verses?

> # There will be times when worry will bust through the door of our hearts and minds, but we always have immediate access to the power to drive worry right back out!

It's worth repeating again that you don't need to beat yourself up if you find yourself worrying. What's more important is that you immediately respond by fighting in faith each time. When you feel one of the four worry drivers, you've got many tools to help you push away from those dangerous attitudes and move toward God.

On the other hand, if you have encountered a difficult or stressful situation and have experienced victory over anxiety or worry, don't move away from that experience but reflect on it! Allow God to show you how fighting in faith got you into position for Him to bring victory in your heart, mind, or life over worry.

Apply It: Tool Tuesday

One of my favorite quotations is from Andy Stanley: "If you don't know why something is working, you won't know how to fix it when it is broken."[6] With that wisdom in mind, today you're going to learn how to do an AAR or an After Action Review. Just as the Israelites have finished the conquest phase of their move into the Promised Land, you have finished four weeks of this Bible study and are moving through the fifth week—and I pray that you have conquered some worry in your life.

This AAR is not a tool of judgment; it is meant to help you identify what you are doing that's working so that the next time you find yourself in a worry battle, you can recall this tool and move forward in victory again. It also may help you remember a few stories that you can share with family and friends about how God has given you victory in your worry battle.

Recall a time recently when you were battling worry, and respond to the following questions:

What worry battle(s) was I fighting? **What was I worrying about the most?** →	**What results have I seen?** **Where do I see changes in the emotional, spiritual, or physical symptoms of worry?** ↓
↑ **What goals will help me move forward?** **What one or two key things will sustain the victory that I've experienced?**	**What has caused the results that I've seen?** **Can I identify verses, tools, or spiritual disciplines that have driven my results?** ←

Today's Takeaway

If worry comes knocking on our door again, we have immediate access to the power to drive it right back out.

What stories or specific situations come to mind as you complete the After Action Review? List them below. If you can, put a date beside each one, too. I love recording dates because it reminds me of how far I've come when I look back.

Story / Situation   **Date**

Prayer

God, thank You for my victories over worry! Even when some of those victories don't feel like big ones, every victory matters. As I reflect on Your promise to give me victory, don't let me settle for anything less than freedom from worry and any other sin or struggle. You've promised me victory through Jesus Christ, and I want to walk in that victory! Amen.

DAY 3: RECEIVING GOD'S INHERITANCE

Have you ever received an inheritance? Generally, an inheritance is a gift given to a recipient after the death of the item's owner, though sometimes it is given before the owner dies. First Timothy 6:7 tells us, "After all, we brought nothing with us when we came into the world, and we can't take anything with us when we leave it." This verse reminds us that we can't take anything that we've accumulated in our lives with us, so our inheritance is what we leave behind for others.

Did you realize that God has an inheritance for you? While the Israelites received a home in the Promised Land, that physical location was just a symbol of the inheritance that God has prepared for His children. First Peter 1:4 describes our inheritance: "We have a priceless inheritance—an inheritance that is kept in heaven for you, pure and undefiled, beyond the reach of change and decay." Even the most priceless pieces of art or automobiles will eventually decay, but God's gifts to us never will!

In a day and age when people are chasing material excess, let's make it our goal to receive God's best. The good news is that as God's daughters, we are His heirs—and that means we will inherit what belongs to God. If we think about what God has, it's everything that we could possibly want. God is sovereign over the heavens and the earth, and so all of that is part of our inheritance; but we also are heirs to God's character and power. Everything that God is, He gives to us. Let me ask you a question: Would you rather experience life on your own, or life infused with God's character and power? The answer is obvious!

Your inheritance is waiting, but there is a catch: you must claim it. It has to be accepted, which means you must take possession of it. An inheritance is not fully realized until it is in the hands of the new owner. Though we have already made our way through Joshua 12, today we are going to backtrack to the final verse of Joshua 11, where we read of the Israelites claiming their inheritance, and then move into chapter 13.

Read Joshua 11:23, and fill in the statements below:

1. Joshua fulfilled God's instructions and gave the land as an

_____ to the Israelites.

2. The land had rest from _____.

Imagine with me the first morning that Joshua wakes up without a new battle to fight. Perhaps as he opens his eyes and stretches his arms overhead, he realizes that he doesn't have to meet with his military officers. Instead of jumping up and calling for reports from his officers, I imagine him taking his time getting dressed and enjoying the Israelite equivalent of a leisurely cup of coffee. Later he might have the chance to visit with the families of some of the fighting men and to see the happy looks on their faces now that the fighting years are over.

Read 1 Peter 1:3-5. Though the Israelites received a homeland as an inheritance, we are promised a far better inheritance. Describe it:

What does God's promise to give you an inheritance—even though you struggle at times—tell you about His character and His attitude toward you?

As we move into Joshua 13, we discover a clue about how long Joshua and the Israelites have been at war.

Read Joshua 13:1. What does God say about Joshua's age?

While Joshua's age is not given, the fact that he is an old man means that the army has been fighting for many years. It's hard to pinpoint Joshua's exact age, but if God calls him "very old" (NIV), that's fairly self-explanatory.

God also makes another observation—one that may be difficult for Joshua to hear.

What else does God say in this verse about the state of the Israelites' campaign in the Promised Land?

I wonder if God's observation feels like a blow to Joshua's ego or a weight of embarrassment? After all of that fighting and defeating thirty-one kings, God says that the job He sent Joshua to do is nowhere near finished. So many battles have been won, yet they are far from complete victory.

Although the Israelites have not yet done all of their part, God still has been faithful to His promise.

Read Joshua 13:2-8. What does God say that He will do to the inhabitants already living in the land? (v. 6)

God instructs Joshua to give the land to the Israelites as what? (v. 6)

How many tribes are waiting to receive their inheritance? (v. 7)

Which tribes received their inheritance from Moses before his death? (v. 8)

Where was their inheritance located? (v. 8)

At the beginning of our study, we learned that there were a few tribes that settled east of the Jordan River. These tribes—Manesseh, Gad, and Reuben—received their inheritance from Moses in Numbers 32. There was a specific reason they wanted to separate from the rest of the Israelites and remain east of the Jordan.

Read Numbers 32:1-6 and 16-22, and then answer the following questions:

Which tribes approached Moses about settling east of the Jordan River? (v. 1)

Why did they want to settle there instead of with the other tribes? (v. 1)

What was the agreement that the tribes made with Moses? (vv. 16-19)

Moses agreed to the tribes' requests, giving them permission to settle east of the Jordan. He also gave the half-tribe of Manasseh permission to settle there. However, he gave some final instructions to Eleazer, the priest, and Joshua about the two and one-half tribes.

Read Numbers 32:28-30. What instructions did Moses give?

There were some conditions on their inheritance. The tribes of Gad and Reuben and the half-tribe of Manasseh had to cross the Jordan and fight just the same as the other tribes. The lesson for us is that knowing about an inheritance isn't enough; we have to take it and transfer it into our name so that it is truly ours.

Imagine that an attorney called you today and said, "Your long-lost great-uncle has left you $250,000, but you have to fly to Japan to pick up the

check. Do you want to come over and get it?" For me, the answer to that question is a no-brainer. I'd say, "Make plans to pick me up tomorrow!" Yet when it comes to our faith, how often do we only read or hear about God's promises for our lives but fail to fight for those promises—to act on them by faith—in order to experience them?

Am I saying that God's Word isn't true in your life if you simply speak it—affirm it verbally? No. I'm saying that if you speak it without allowing it to sink in and transform your life through faith-filled action, then you won't experience its full power. When you do your part by faith, God supplies His power. Rather than a name-it-and-claim-it faith, this kind of faith looks at God's promises as an open door to experience more love, hope, joy, and peace—the things that all of the money and possessions in the world cannot buy.

When you do your part by faith, God supplies His power.

The most practical example of this I can think of has to do with finances. I've heard some people say, "I know that God's going to bless my finances. Since God has cattle on a thousand hills, I know that He can pay my bills." Now, it's true that God does have unlimited resources and can take care of all of our needs. But are we fighting or working to realize those promises in our lives? If we refuse to work or choose to recklessly spend our income, then we're positioning ourselves for scarcity instead of God's power. And often the blessing is not in any material or tangible outcome but in God's abundant provision for our spiritual needs. Rather than the security of having financial wealth, many receive the deep riches that come from walking by faith and trusting Him. In any case, whenever God wants to give us something, whether tangible or intangible, He grants us the wisdom to get in position for it.

When it comes to our finances, God gives us wise money management advice such as:

- Avoid accumulating debt that you can't pay (Proverbs 22:7).
- Honor God with the first fruits of your increase (Malachi 3:10; Matthew 23:23).
- Don't fall in love with money (1 Timothy 6:10).
- Live generously (2 Corinthians 9:6).

These are just some of the ways we can get into position to experience God's promises related to His provision for us. But again, it's important to remember that we should puruse a rich, satisfying relationship with God instead of expecting Him to shower us with riches.

What is a promise or blessing of God that you are ready to receive or experience in your life?

What's the difference between *knowing* **that you have a promise or inheritance and actually** *claiming* **or** *receiving* **it?**

We can learn a lot from the attitude of the tribes of Gad and Reuben about claiming inheritances. Like Joshua, those men were willing to fight for the land that God promised. Sweet friend, the enemy of our souls will do everything possible to discourage us from receiving the heavenly treaures we've been promised, including the help and support of our three fighting friends. As the Scriptures confirm, he is an accuser who will tell us that we're unworthy of God's best and who will condemn us when we fall. But as God's heirs, claiming our inheritance does not depend on our worthiness; rather, we can claim our inheritance because God has given His word and promise to us!

Apply It: Wisdom Wednesday

An unclaimed gift is an unwanted gift.

Prayer

God, I am so grateful that You love giving gifts! No only did You give me Jesus Christ to rescue me from sin and death, but You also have given me the fighting friends of Peace, Courage, and Strength so that I can experience Your victory over my struggles. And even more than these lavish blessings, You have an eternal inheritance awaiting me! Thank You, God, for being such a loving gift-giver. I put my trust in You! Amen.

DAY 4: GOD REDEEMS

Now that the Promised Land has rest from war, it's time for the tribes to know what areas they will occupy. But this is quite a task to complete! There are a number of chapters in the Book of Joshua that discuss how the inheritance is to be distributed (Joshua 13–18). We are covering most of the land distribution in this week's study and will finish at the beginning of next week. Rather than each tribe rushing to a section of land and staking a claim, Joshua implements the plan that God gave Moses (Numbers 34–35).

Today we will consider two unique twists to the allotment process. First, there is a tribe that does not receive an allotment. And second, the descendants of one of Jacob's sons will receive not one but two inheritance allotments.

Let's begin by talking about the tribe that is not receiving an allotment. As we have been looking at the map of Canaan throughout our study (page 11), you might have wondered why the tribe of Levi is not shown. We're going to unpack

the explanation and discover a great lesson that we can apply to our lives today.

Numbers 18 captures the list of duties of the Levites, which primarily center around the care of the religious duties.

Read Numbers 18:20-21. What does God tell Aaron about the Levite land allotment?

And the Levites were given no land at all, only towns to live in with surrounding pasturelands for their livestock and all their possessions.

(Joshua 14:4b)

What will the Levites receive as an inheritance instead of land?

God Himself will be the inheritance for the Levites, and He promises to provide for them by giving them the tithes [offerings] of Israel. This is the provision given before they enter the Promised Land; yet when it is time to settle into the land, God makes another special provision for the Levites.

Read Joshua 13:14. How else will God provide for the Levites?

² [The leaders of the tribe of Levi] came to them at Shiloh in the land of Canaan and said, "The Lord commanded Moses to give us towns to live in and pasturelands for our livestock." ³ So by the command of the Lord the people of Israel gave the Levites the following towns and pasturelands out of their own grants of land.

(Joshua 21:2-3)

While the Levites won't have their own designated land inheritance, God does provide places for them to live.

Read Joshua 14:4b and 21:2-3 in the margin. Rather than an assigned land inheritance, the Levites will live in various cities. Who gives the Levites these places to live?

The Israelites give of their own land inheritance to the Levites, so that the Levites are living among the people throughout the Promised Land. Next week we will discuss a certain category of cities given to the Levites. But the fact that the Levites are assigned specific cities within the territories allotted to each tribe of Israel fulfills words spoken by their ancestor Jacob centuries before.

Read Genesis 49:5-7. As Jacob neared the end of his life, he gathered his sons in order to prophesy about their future and his descendants.

What curse did Jacob give Levi? (v. 7)

Why did Jacob pronounce this curse? (v. 6)

Jacob's prophecy, given in response to the murderous revenge of his sons Levi and Simeon (see Genesis 34), now comes true as the Levites are scattered throughout the Promised Land. (In fact, because the Levites do not receive their own land inheritance, the tribe of Levi is omitted from many lists of the twelve tribes of Israel. See the "Extra Insight" on page 162.) Yet this curse actually becomes a blessing for the Levites and all of Israel.[7] Rather than being consolidated in one solitary tribe away from all the other tribes, the Levites are interspersed throughout all of the tribes—taking the religious traditions with them and symbolizing God's presence within their communities.

Thinking about how God redeemed Levi's savage revenge-murder generations later gives me hope. When I reflect on my greatest worry battles, I realize that those battles have become touchstones of faith in my life. They mark moments in my life when I had to learn how to fight in faith so I would no longer experience the horrible meltdowns that come with extreme worry. And they mark victories that are spread out over every area of my life. I've not only won worry battles over my hopes and dreams; I've won worry battles related to parenting, marriage, finances, my career, and more.

Take a moment to reflect on your life. Check the areas of your life where you've battled worry. Then check those areas where you've experienced a victory. (The battle and victory may or may not have happened consecutively or they may not even be the same situation.)

	WORRY BATTLE	VICTORY
Mental/Emotional Struggle	_____	_____
Dating/Marriage	_____	_____
Health	_____	_____
Parenting	_____	_____
Career	_____	_____
Finances	_____	_____

The Twelve Tribes of Israel: Reuben, Simeon, Judah, Zebulun, Issachar, Dan, Gad, Asher, Naphtali, Benjamin, Manasseh, Ephraim

Are there any victorious moments that come to mind as you reflect?

What did it feel like to know that God gave you victory to beat back worry and live worry-free in that situation or situations?

Now that we've considered the first twist to the allotment process—the inheritance of the Levites—we're ready for the second twist. The descendants of one of Jacob's sons would receive not one but two inheritance allotments. We touched on the reason for this in the Introduction to the Book of Joshua (pages 8–10), but now we're going to take a closer look.

Compare the list of the twelve tribes of Israel in the margin with the list of Jacob's sons found in Genesis 49:1-28. Other than Levi, which son's name is missing from the twelve tribes of Israel?

Now read Genesis 48:3-6. Jacob is speaking to Joseph about Joseph's two sons. What are their names?

What does Jacob tell Joseph about his two sons and their future inheritance?

Jacob, whose name God changed to Israel, adopted Joseph's sons, Ephraim and Manasseh, as his own. (This is why many lists of the twelve tribes of Israel replace Joseph with Manesseh and Ephraim.) This meant that when the Israelites took possession of the Promised Land, the descendants of Joseph's two sons would receive a land inheritance, just as the descendants of Joseph's brothers would. Yet when it came time to actually assign land to Joseph's sons, things were a little tricky. As we've already learned, Moses gave half of the tribe of Manasseh an inheritance east of the Jordan River. And the other half of the tribe of Manasseh, as well as the the tribe of Ephraim, were deeply concerned about their inheritance on the western side of the Jordan.

Read Joshua 17:14-18. What, specifically, are the tribes of Ephraim and Manasseh concerned about?

What does Joshua tell them to do?

On the Map

Locate Manesseh and Ephraim on the western side of the Jordan River (page 11).

Centuries before, Jacob had prophesied that Joseph's descendants would be numerous, and that certainly has come true. But now the two tribes are worried that they won't have enough land. They also express concern that the Canaanites have iron chariots, symbols of battle strength.

Rather than try to arrive at a fancy solution or succumb to the tribes' complaints, Joshua sticks with God's plan. He presents the two tribes with the same instructions that God gave the entire nation of Israel, telling them that they are strong enough to fight for their land, remove the inhabitants, and claim it as their own.

There are times when we think that our problems are special and, therefore, that few others could understand our complex predicament. Often when we're sharing our worry with someone, we find ourselves using the phrase, "But you don't understand..."

Sometimes we take that same tone with God. When we have a worry before us, we may think that God's wisdom falls short of our situation. But it never does.

Read 1 Corinthians 1:25 in the margin. How does God's wisdom compare to our human wisdom?

This foolish plan of God is wiser than the wisest of human plans, and God's weakness is stronger than the greatest of human strength.
(1 Corinthians 1:25)

Once we feel a little victory under our belts in the battle against worry, the temptation can be to put our own unique twist on God's wisdom. It's like when someone teaches you to cook a particular recipe: you follow their instructions to the teaspoon for the first few times that you make the meal; but after you get comfortable with the process, you begin to customize the recipe to your own personal flavor.

Spiritually speaking, I know this happens to me. When I first began to intensely battle worry, I memorized verse after verse of God's promises. Goodness, I soaked in hours of Bible study and prayer, desperately clinging to whatever God would teach me! I would begin to fight in faith and experience victory over worry. All of a sudden I would feel extra excitement and energy.

But then I'd take those good feelings and begin to chase after other things that often squeezed out my time with God. Before long, a resurgence of worry or an attack of panic would be just the motivation I needed to get back on track.

It took a long time for me to realize that if I was going to face fresh worries each day, then I would need a fresh word from God each day to help me make my way. I've learned that I can celebrate victory over worry without losing focus spiritually.

When you experience victory over worry and think that future battles won't require the same amount of effort, remember Joshua's words to the tribes of Ephraim and Manesseh.

"Clear as much of the land as you wish, and take possession of its farthest corners. And you will drive out the Canaanites from the valleys, too, even though they are strong and have iron chariots."

(Joshua 17:18)

Read Joshua 17:18 in the margin. How do you think this verse translates to your worry battle?

Even though the tribes of Manasseh and Ephraim fought alongside Joshua and the Israelites all of those years, there were still more battles to be fought. Joshua reminded them that they could claim all that they were promised and more, but they had to do the work. Victory would be theirs if they fought for it.

Here's the application for us: We can clear out all of the worry in our lives by fighting in faith; and when we apply those same faith tools in other struggles, we can be victorious in those areas of our lives as well. Regardless of our enemy or our enemy's resources, God will give us victory over all!

Apply It: Temperature Check Thursday

It's that time of the week for you to think about how your worry battle is progressing. Don't beat yourself up if you're battling some extra worries this week; by the same token, make sure to give yourself credit if you have been fighting in faith and God's power has given you victory.

Circle the number that indicates where you are today:

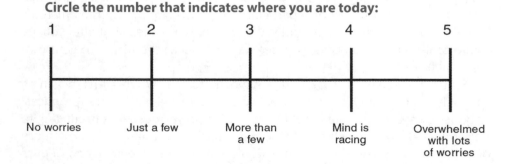

1	2	3	4	5
No worries	Just a few	More than a few	Mind is racing	Overwhelmed with lots of worries

If you've circled 1-2, what promises, disciplines, or practices do you attribute with putting you in position to handle worry well?

If you've circled 3, 4, or 5, are you struggling with a new worry or has something changed? How can you renew your focus on training up your fighting friends?

What is a specific next step that you need to take or a commitment that you need to make?

Today's Takeaway

Whatever spiritual victory I have experienced remains mine as long as I remain in God's presence.

Prayer

Dear God, as I think about where I am in my battle against worry, I give thanks that Your promise for victory always stands. Help me to remember that every battle won over victory reinforces my faith for future battles. I also give thanks that You can take my worry-weary past and redeem it for Your glory and my blessing. Amen.

DAY 5: "WELL DONE, GOOD AND FAITHFUL SERVANT"

This week we're learning from the Israelites as they claim their inheritance and receive their victory. Today we're going to narrow the focus to an individual and catch up with Caleb, who stood with Joshua against the other ten spies after the first scouting expedition into the land of Canaan decades earlier. Now it's time for Caleb to receive his blessing for a lifetime of faithfulness. It's people like Caleb who encourage me to fight for faithfulness each day of my life, even when no one is paying attention—because God always is!

Before we get to Caleb's inheritance, let's begin with the first tribe to receive an inheritance west of the Jordan—and we'll see a conection a little later. We've talked about two twists or special circumstances in the land allotment process, but now it's time to get down to business!

The first tribe to receive their allotment of land west of the Jordan is the tribe of Judah (Joshua 15). With its eastern border running along the Dead Sea and its western border along the Mediterranean Sea, Judah is the most southern and largest allotment of land in Canaan.

Turn to the map on page 11, and locate Judah. What famous city is located here, and why is it famous?

That's right: Bethlehem. Located in the northeastern section of Judah, this city was the birthplace of Jesus. Here's another interesting observation. As you look again at the map on page 11, notice that the tribe of Simeon has land smack in the middle of Judah. It's the only tribe to receive an allotment within another tribe's inheritance.

Read Joshua 19:1-9. What reason is given for the tribe of Simeon's inheritance to be in that specific location?

Although the tribe of Judah is large in population, they still have more land area than they need; so the tribe of Simeon is assigned a portion in the midst of Judah's territory. Notice that, in these verses, no land boundaries are identified, unlike the land inheritances of the other tribes. All that is included is a list of the cities given to them. A possible explanation can be traced back to a passage that we touched on yesterday.

Look again at Genesis 49:5-7. What is a possible explanation for why the tribe of Simeon has an allotment without boundaries within the territory of Judah?

The other tribes are assigned their land inheritances (Joshua 14:1-2). Then, once those are finished, Caleb arrives to pay Joshua a visit.

Read Joshua 14:6-9, and answer the following questions:

How old was Caleb when Moses sent him and the other men to spy on Canaan? (v. 7)

Even though the Israelites' hearts melted in fear, what does Caleb say about himself? (v. 8)

What did Moses prophesy about Caleb's future inheritance? (v. 9)

I can see Caleb coming to stand before Joshua, the only other man to survive the wilderness for forty years. I imagine the two men looking at each other eye to eye. While there's no record of how often they have seen each other in the years since arriving in Canaan, there's no doubt that their shared history still plays loudly in their memories.

Both men saw the Promised Land before anyone else, including Moses. Both men witnessed an entire assembly of people rise up and threaten to kill them. Both men watched as, one by one, every other adult they knew died in the wilderness. And both had responsibilities related to the distribution of the Promised Land.

Read Numbers 34:16-19, 29 and answer the following:

What is Joshua assigned to do (along with Eleazar the priest)? (v. 17)

What tribe does Caleb belong to? (v. 19)

What has Caleb been assigned to do? (vv. 18-19, 29)

As the leader assigned to assist in the division of land among the families of the tribe of Judah, Caleb would have quite a task assigning individual plots of land to individual families. Yet despite this significant responsibility, Caleb takes time to go to Joshua to claim a promise made to him long ago.

Read Joshua 14:10-14. How old is Caleb at the time he presents himself to Joshua to claim his inheritance? (v. 10)

How does he describe his physical health? (v. 11)

For whatever reason, I envision Caleb resembling an aged Rocky Balboa, the professional boxing champion in the popular "Rocky" movies. I don't know if Caleb filled out a muscle shirt at eighty-five, but the fact that he says he could fight like he was in his forties is impressive!

I'm drawn to watching and listening to older adults who maintain their physical health. Yes, genetics is definitely important, but there's something compelling about Earnestine Shepherd, a body-builder who turned eighty-one in June 2017, or Johanna Quaas, a German gymnast in her nineties who holds the official title "World's Oldest Gymnast"[8] and whose gymnastic routine on the bars went viral. Like Caleb, these women are more than just strong; they have a fire within that gives them courage to keep fighting for their passion, even at a time in life when others might want them to sit back and watch the world go by.

Who is someone of a mature age that you admire for his or her passion and faith? Describe what you admire about this person:

Without a doubt, Caleb had the kind of faith and passion we all aspire to have in our older years.

What does Caleb ask Joshua for? (v. 12)

What does he say he will do to the Anakites living there? (v. 12)

What city does Joshua give to Caleb? (v. 13)

Turn again to the map on page 11, and locate Hebron in the territory of Judah. Hebron is a city whose name means "to join."[9] This has rich symbolic meaning when we think of Caleb's life. His faithfulness drives him to serve God wholeheartedly. Caleb makes God's priorities his priorities. Throughout his life, Caleb joins with God and is rewarded.

I love how Caleb isn't afraid to step out and claim his inheritance. How many of us are afraid to take what God wants to give us and put our name on it? That has been the case many times in my own life.

One year in late December, I was sitting in the living room of my childhood home and thinking about returning to campus for the second half of my freshman year of college. Christmas break was almost over, and I didn't have

enough money to pay for my books. I worried about how to stretch the little bit of money that I had earned over break into the hundreds of dollars I needed for books.

My dad walked in and sat down in the chair opposite mine. He asked, "So, do you need book money?"

My eyes got big. I was terrified that if I admitted I didn't have book money, my dad might tell me that I needed to stay home and work during the winter semester to save money. Instead, he pulled out a hundred dollar bill, put it on the coffee table, and asked, "Is this enough?"

Again, I didn't know what to say. Was this a trick?

Dad pulled out another hundred dollar bill. "Is this enough?"

By this point, I was crying.

He pulled out one more hundred dollar bill and placed it next to the other bills. "Is this enough?"

I nodded my head.

He handed me the money and waited until I could look him in the eye. All he said was, "Why didn't you ask for book money?"

How often do we fret about things instead of talking to God about them before they become a fountain of worry in our lives?

Read James 4:2-3 in the margin. What are the two reasons that we don't have what we want?

Reason #1:

Reason #2:

What have you been afraid to ask God for lately?

How has your lack of courage to ask God for it caused you to worry?

²You want what you don't have, so you scheme and kill to get it. You are jealous of what others have, but you can't get it, so you fight and wage war to take it away from them. Yet you don't have what you want because you don't ask God for it. ³And even when you ask, you don't get it because your motives are all wrong—you want only what will give you pleasure.

(James 4:2-3)

We've got to stop saying "no" to things that we haven't asked God for yet. We're putting words in God's mouth when we assume He will say "no" to something before we ask. While God's not a divine vending machine and He doesn't make deals, God does love being generous. And He invites us to be bold and generous, too. We learn this not only from Caleb but also from his daughter.

In Joshua 15, there's a little sliver of a story about Caleb's daughter, Aksah (Acsah, NLT), and her bold ask of her father—and the even bigger "yes" that she

received. This story has really challenged me to think bigger about what I'm willing to ask of God.

Read Joshua 15:16-19, and answer the following questions:

What was the offer Caleb made to any man who would fight and capture Debir (Kiriath Sepher)?

What did Aksah ask her father to give her, even after her husband had asked for a new field on her behalf?

How did Caleb respond?

> **To be victorious in the worry battle, we must worry less about God saying no if we make the "big ask."**

Though her name is spelled differently in various translations, I like the simplicity of Aksah in the New International Version. And every time I see that spelling, my mind transposes the letters and reads "ask." She reminds me of the importance of not fearing the "big ask."

Write a prayer about something you've been hesitant to ask God for. Unlike last week when we talked about "sun stand still" prayers for the impossible, this doesn't have to be something that seems impossible but simply something that is deeply important to your heart. Whatever it is, write your prayer below:

To be victorious in the worry battle, we must worry less about God saying no if we make the "big ask." Trust is essential for a life of freedom. But for many of us, what we fear more than the thought of God saying "no" is the possibility that He may answer our prayers in a way that we don't want. When we're struggling with that fear, we need to remember the following verses.

Read 1 John 3:1 and Matthew 7:11 in the margin.

What kind of love does God pour out on His children?

What kind of gifts does God give to His children?

See how very much our Father loves us, for he calls us his children, and that is what we are!

(1 John 3:1)

So if you sinful people know how to give good gifts to your children, how much more will your heavenly Father give good gifts to those who ask him.

(Matthew 7:11)

Yes! God only knows how to give good gifts to His children. Yet if you are in the midst of a tragic or painful life circumstance that is keeping you awake at night, it can be hard to see the good. However, God's goodness isn't about a small window of time; it's much bigger than our perspective. God sees and knows your pain, but He's also saying to you, "Don't you worry, my beloved child. Wait until you see what I've got for you." As Romans 8:28 assures us, God will work all things for the good of those who love Him and are called according to His purpose. Because that is something we can count on, let us dare to ask big!

Apply It: Freedom Friday

This week we've been talking about claiming our inheritance, and today we've tied a ribbon around it by focusing on God's generosity and our need to pray bold, big prayers. You may be struggling with guilt if you don't think that you are worthy enough to make a bold ask of God. On this Freedom Friday, I want you to meditate on 1 John 3:1 and Matthew 7:11, because guilt should never keep you, God's dearly loved child, from being like Aksah and making a bold request of your Father. Remember, He delights to lavish you with love and good gifts!

If you didn't write a prayer on the previous page, here's one more opportunity for you to make a bold ask of God. If you did write a prayer, summarize your request below with a phrase or word:

Today's Takeaway

God loves it when His children make big asks in accordance with His bold promises!

Prayer

God, I want to be like Caleb—to follow You wholeheartedly even when others run away in fear. I want to live a bold, vibrant life of faithfulness so that even in my old age I will have the energy to continue to fight in faith for whatever comes my way. I also pray with the boldness of Caleb's daughter, Aksah, asking you for _____. It's a big ask, God, but You are a big God, and nothing is too great for You. So, I make this request, and I leave the answer in Your hands. I will continue to fight in faith and not worry about anything today, because You are with me and I do not have to fear. In Jesus' name, Amen.

Joshua 13:1—Much remains to be conquered

Joshua 13:6—God's promise to drive out the Israelites' enemies

We're always going to _____ worry. . . .

And rather than beat ourselves up [when we worry], we remember God's _____ and

His _____.

God's plan for success: *Joshua 1:8*

God's definition of victory: When we believe that God is with us and for us in every

circumstance real or imagined.

Reasons we get tired of battling worry:

1. _____   3. _____

2. _____   4. _____

The Israelites did not _____ _____ _____.

We can always get _____ _____ the battle.

We never have to settle for less than _____ _____.

Joshua 14:10-12—Caleb's request

We never get too _____ to fight for God's best for us.

Joshua 15:19—The request of Caleb's daughter

Matthew 7:11—Our heavenly Father gives good gifts to those who ask

Numbers 27:5-10—Zelophehad's daughters

Claiming your inheritance as a child of God isn't a blessing just for you, but _____

will be _____ as well.

Galatians 6:9—Do not grow weary of doing good.

See page 206 for answers.

WEEK
6

AMEN!

Living in Victory

Joshua 18–24

MEMORY VERSE

"You are a witness to your own decision. . . . You have chosen to serve the LORD."
(Joshua 24:22)

Well, my friend, we've made it to the final week of our journey through the Book of Joshua! In the Introduction to the Book of Joshua on pages 8–10, I've identified four phases of the book: arrival, acquisition, allotment, and allegiance. This week we'll be in chapters 18–24, and at this point, most of the tribes are in a holding pattern during the allotment phase. They've been assigned their inheritance, but since they haven't been obedient to God's command to completely drive out the enemy, they aren't experiencing the total and promised victory. As we examine this part of their story, we'll discover that some of those worry drivers—weariness, compromise, apathy, and doubt—are undermining the Israelites' pursuit of all that God has promised them. And we'll see how one group of Israelites chooses concern over worry and confronts another group in a positive way, serving as a good example for us when we are worried about someone in our lives.

By the way, the story of the Israelites' settling into the Promised Land doesn't end with the final chapter of the Book of Joshua. If you will keep reading through the Old Testament historical books, such as Judges, you'll discover whether all twelve tribes eventually claim their victory.

Here's what I want you to remember: Even after this study ends, God's promise to give you victory over worry remains. Experiencing victory and holding on to victory result from the same strategy: fighting in faith. Never let a worry discourage you, friend. Instead, always see worry as an opportunity to fight in faith and experience God's sweet victory! And to that I'll add an "Amen!"

As a young girl, I went to a black church where I wore patent leather shoes and swang my feet as I sat in a wood pew listening to the people shout "Amen!" whenever the preacher said something they liked. The word *amen* means "so let it be."[1] When it comes to your worry battle, my prayer is that victory will be true in your life as you continue to activate your fighting friends Peace, Courage, and Strength and use the tools you've learned on a regular basis. Most of all, I pray you will have some great stories to tell about how God is giving you victory over worry. So I say a big "Amen!" to your desire to keep battling worry and experiencing God's victory. Let me say it again: "Amen!"

DAY 1: WHAT ARE YOU WAITING FOR?

As we begin our week of study in Joshua 18, Joshua gives the people a stern reprimand. Picture this: the entire nation of Israel meets at Shiloh, which is located on the mid-eastern side of Ephraim. Though a number of the twelve tribes have already received allotments, it is important for the Israelites to remember their unity as a people instead of running after their individual interests.

Read Joshua 18:2-5. What have they not done yet?

Since the people have not gone to claim the remaining inheritances, Joshua decides to send scouts into the land to survey it and then write a report on what they see.

Read Joshua 18:6. How will Joshua divide the land?

God had instructed Moses in the process of dividing the land before the Israelites entered the Promised Land.

Read Numbers 26:52-56, where God gives Moses instructions about how to distribute the land inheritances.

Circle the statement that is true in each pair:

The tribes can select whatever land fits their fancy.

The land is to be divided with specific boundaries.

Allotments are based on the population of tribe. Bigger tribes receive more land.

All tribes receive the same size allotment, no matter their numbers.

Moses hands out lotto tickets.

Lots are cast to assign the specific locations.

Why did God tell Moses to assign the land by lots? Casting lots appears many times in Scripture and for a variety of purposes. In the Old Testament, casting lots was considered to be the way to reveal God's supernatural designation in specific circumstances. There are only a few instances in the New Testament where lots are cast, including the soldiers casting lots for Jesus' clothes (Matthew 27:35; Mark 15:24; John 19:23-24) and the disciples casting lots to choose Judas's replacement after Jesus' ascension into heaven (Acts 1:22-26). After Matthias was chosen as the new apostle on the Day of Pentecost, the use of casting lots isn't mentioned again.[3]

Read Proverbs 16:33 in the margin. Even though a lot is cast, who determines the decision?

"The lot is cast into the lap,
*   but its every decision*
*   is from the LORD."*
*   (Proverbs 16:33 NIV)*

Now read Joshua 18:9-10. What does Joshua do once the men return with their descriptions of the land?

Joshua begins to cast lots, but it is God who assigns the territories to the individual tribes as their inheritance. Joshua 19 records the allotments to the tribe of Simeon, which we discussed in last week's study, as well as those to the tribes of Issachar, Asher, Naphtali, and Dan. Though the chapter records the cities and boundaries of the first four tribes, we discover a little more detail about what happens to the tribe of Dan as they attempt to settle their land. They receive an allotment on the westernmost side of the Promised Land, with the port city of Joppa named among the cities. Yet this is not actually where the people of Dan will wind up settling.

Read Joshua 19:47. What happens when the people of Dan try to drive the people from their land?

This verse summarizes a very interesting and troubling story. In fact, it's worth taking a closer look.

When the people of Dan try to claim their land, the Amorites take up arms and push the people of Dan back. As much as we'd like to know why the tribe of Dan retreats and fails to advance again to claim their inheritance, Scripture doesn't say. Instead, the tribe of Dan later hatches a new plan to take over a different area that God did not assign to them.

So far, what do the actions of the tribe of Dan say about their faith in God's promises?

We find the rest of the story in Judges 18, and it's quite a tale. A little background is helpful before we jump into the text.

In Judges 17, we're introduced to a man named Micah from the tribe of Ephraim. We meet Micah as he confesses stealing 1,100 pieces of silver from his mother. She is so grateful that he has admitted to stealing the money and has returned it that she takes a portion of the silver and has idols made from the precious metal. Then a young Levite named Jonathan travels north from his home in Bethlehem (in Judah) and ends up traveling through Ephraim. Micah runs into Jonathan and invites him to stay within his own home. When he finds out that Jonathan is a Levite, Micah hires Jonathan as his own personal rent-a-priest for ten pieces of silver per year (probably his mother's money).

With that background, let's look at Judges 18, where the tribe of Dan comes into the story.

Read Judges 18:1-2. How many men from the tribe of Dan are sent to scout out land?

The people of Dan are basically homeless. Frankly, it is their own fault. I'm curious about the tribal leaders and why they have failed to fight and claim God's promises. Instead of fighting to claim the land that they've been given, the leaders of Dan decide to find a new city in which to settle. The first verse of Judges 18 explains how they can hatch such a plan with no accountability: "Now in those days Israel had no king."

At this point in the story, Joshua is dead, and the Israelites have no leader or king who is accountable to God's leading. Instead, there are a series of judges. Five men of the tribe of Dan who are living in the eastern hills of the territory allotted to their tribe travel north and end up at Micah's house in Ephraim. They meet the young priest, Jonathan, and ask him to inquire of God on their behalf.

Read Judges 18:5-6. What do the men want the priest to ask God?

Is there any mention that he actually talks to God?

When they ask Jonathan the priest to consult God about their upcoming mission, he gives them the affirmative on their pursuit, even though there is no record of him consulting with God. The men end up selecting the city of Laish in the territory of the tribe of Naphtali as their target. This city is the northernmost city in the Promised Land and a very long way from their God-given inheritance.

Read Judges 18:7. What do the men observe about the town and people of Laish?

The people of Laish are described as carefree, peaceful, secure, and wealthy (Judges 18:7). How can this be if the tribe of Naphtali is supposed to be about the business of removing all of the original inhabitants of the land as God instructed? It turns out that Naphtali is one of the tribes that has failed to drive out the Canaanites, as recorded in Judges 1. So, it seems that the people of Laish have forgotten all about the threat of the Israelites.

Read Judges 18:27-31. After killing everyone in Laish, what does the tribe of Dan rename the town?

What does the tribe of Dan do that God specifically prohibited?

The Danite warriors easily defeat the people of Laish and take over the territory for themselves, renaming it Dan. However, we find in the very next chapter a heartbreaking story of idol-worship and pay-for-hire priests—all of which is contradictory to God's instructions related to defeating their enemies and living victoriously in the Promised Land. You might say that the tribe of Dan's conquest is an example of a bad victory.

Now, let's return to the land allotments in the Book of Joshua and turn our attention to the uplifting and inspiring account of Joshua's allotment. Yes, the leader of the Israelites receives an allotment, too. What's inspiring is not that Joshua is rewarded but when and how he receives his award.

Read Joshua 19:49-51. What had God said that Joshua could have, and who gives it to him?

Today I will fight in faith and trust my future to God.

What city does Joshua choose? Where is it located?

It's important to note that, as the leader of the campaign into the Promised Land, Joshua could have stood up at the start of the land allotments and said, "Me first!" But he didn't. It wasn't until all of the land had been given that Joshua selected his inheritance. This is the mark of a true servant leader—after the example of Jesus.

As you know, Joshua is one of my personal heroes. He was an imperfect man who wholeheartedly followed God and stewarded his leadership gifts well. As a result, God blessed Joshua with many victories and a powerful influence throughout the land of Canaan.

Do you realize that a similar thing might happen to you? As you grow stronger in courage and strength, you'll have the faith to take on bigger and bigger assignments from God. At some point, people in your sphere of influence might begin to notice. God might even open up opportunities outside your sphere of influence. This is when it's good to remember another key element of Joshua's charater: humility.

Even as Joshua demonstrated tremendous humility, Jesus is our perfect example of humility.

Read Ephesians 2:5-9. What are the humble attitudes that Christ modeled for us?

As you begin to experience great victories over worry, how can you demonstrate Christlike humility when others commend you on acts of great faith, personal achievements, or your growing influence?

Today's Takeaway

I don't have to settle for less than God's best.

As I think about today's study, I realize how much you and I need the examples of men like Joshua and women like the daughters of Zelophehad (Joshua 17:3-6). Both are humble, faithful, and courageous examples of trusting God's promises even when times are hard and the odds are against us. Each day we can take a step toward being like Joshua and the daughters of Zelophehad when we say, "Today I will fight in faith and trust my future to God."

Apply It: Monday Motivation

"Sometimes we are afraid to reach out and live the life that we believe that we have been called to. But fear is no friend. It may seem to protect, but it slowly suffocates."[4]
—*Sheila Walsh*

Prayer

God, thank You for Joshua's example of humility in the face of great faithfulness and victory. As You give me victory over worry, may I never forget that You are the source of my victory. Amen.

DAY 2: SAFE PLACES

God thinks of everything! Even as the Promised Land is the new home of the Israelites, God acknowledges that not everything will be perfect in their new residence. So God sets up safeguards to protect the people from some of the consequences of our broken world and prevent needless worry when an unspeakable accident happens.

Read Joshua 20:1-3. Why does God instruct the people to establish cities of refuge?

One commentator called the environment at that time a "blood-for-blood" culture.[5] To combat rogue revenge-seeking behavior, God made provision for cities of refuge for those who might accidentally kill another person.

What example is given in Deuteronomy 19:5 for why a person might need a city of refuge?

Though the people didn't have the complex legal laws that govern our courts today, they did have a structure for the cities of refuge and a defined due process.

Read Joshua 20:4-6 and answer the following questions:

A person seeking refuge would have to stand at the entrance of the city and do what?

If the avenging family shows up to retaliate, what are the elders/leaders not to do?

Extra Insight

Deuteronomy 16:18-20 tells of the appointment of judges and officials in all of the tribes. They were to be fair, never showing partiality or accepting bribes.

So let us come boldly to the throne of our gracious God. There we will receive his mercy, and we will find grace to help us when we need it most.

(Hebrews 4:16)

Christ suffered for our sins once for all time. He never sinned, but he died for sinners to bring you safely home to God. He suffered physical death, but he was raised to life in the Spirit.

(1 Peter 3:18)

My dear children, I am writing this to you so that you will not sin. But if anyone does sin, we have an advocate who pleads our case before the Father. He is Jesus Christ, the one who is truly righteous. ² He himself is the sacrifice that atones for our sins—and not only our sins but the sins of all the world.

(1 John 2:1-2)

Where is the trial to take place, and how long are they to stay there?

In Deuteronomy 4, we see that Moses chose three cities of refuge on the eastern side of the Jordan. The people of Israel affirmed those cities and then chose three more cities on the western side of the Jordan.

Read Joshua 20:7-9 and fill in the blanks below. You will need to refer to the map on page 11 in order to determine the locations.

Eastern Cities of Refuge	Western Cities of Refuge
1. _____	1. _____
2. _____	2. _____
3. _____	3. _____

You'll notice that the Israelites strategically chose cities in the northern, middle, and southern areas of the Promised Land. Additionally, they chose to divide the cities equally on both sides of the Jordan.

In a spiritual sense, we need a place of refuge, too, a place where we find forgiveness from sin; and because of Jesus, we have that place.

Read Hebrews 4:16 in the margin. Where are we to go boldly and receive mercy and grace in our time of need?

What do 1 Peter 3:18 and 1 John 2:1-2 (in the margin) tell us about how Jesus made this possible?

Those cities of refuge remind me of the work of Jesus on the cross that makes it possible for us to have access to the throne of our gracious God, where we find mercy. Though our sin and mistakes have caused pain, heartache, and loss, our Savior rescues us from sin and offers us a place of refuge through forgiveness.

During my sophomore year of college, I became pregnant. When I saw the two lines on that pregnancy test, I put the pedal to the metal on worry and revved from zero to meltdown in less than six seconds. As a Christ-follower, I knew that I had sinned by choosing my way instead of God's way, and the weight of that sin and my own self-condemnation crushed my soul.

When I woke up a few days later, my only option seemed to be running away. In fact, I contacted a childhood friend who lived across the country and began making arrangements to move away from my family. Looking back, it seems so silly now. But at the time, I thought that I could run from God by moving across the country.

A couple of weeks later, I was sitting in my dorm room, worn out from worry and guilt. I slid off my bed onto my knees and began to pray. It was in that moment that my heart cried out for God's grace and refuge at the time I needed it most.

There have been many times in my life when I've thrown my hands up in the air and collapsed onto the floor, crying out God's name. While my circumstances may have anguished my heart, the fact that I could fall on my face before God and cry out for help soothes my soul.

When you come to God for help, He won't turn you away. If you fear God's condemnation for your failures, remember the truth of Romans 8:1, which tells us that God's children are never condemned because Jesus' sacrifice freed them from condemnation. You are free to run to God right now!

Do you need to come boldly to God's throne of grace today and ask for mercy or forgiveness? Write a prayer below and offer it up to God:

Last week, we learned that the Levites weren't to receive a specific land allotment but would be assigned specific cities throughout the Promised Land.

Read Joshua 21:41. How many cities were the Levites assigned throughout the Promised Land?

Joshua 21 closes with a definitive statement that not only summarizes the end of the Israelites' campaign to win and settle the Promised Land but that also captures an essential truth of God's character.

Write Joshua 21:45 below, and circle the word *all*.

Extra Insight

Within the tribe of Levi, there were multiple clan families who were assigned to specific cities. The names of those clan families are listed in Numbers 26, along with the other tribes' clan families.

Today's Takeaway

Even when I'm unfaithful, God never fails to be faithful to me.

Centuries have passed since the time God entered into a covenant with Abraham to give him many descendants and bring his future family into a land of their own. Not only did God keep that promise, but God also kept His promises to Moses both before and after the Israelites were released from slavery—as well as His promises to Joshua when the Israelites entered the Promised Land. God kept all of His promises!

Isn't it compelling to realize that God kept His promises even though, as we've read many times, God's people did not always keep their end of the agreement? Despite their unfaithfulness, God was still faithful!

My sister, this is why we must always fight in faith! Though we may fall down from time to time in our battle against worry or any other threat in our life, God always, always keeps His promises to us. He will never fail us!

Apply It: Tool Tuesday

Over the past six weeks you've acquired many tools that can equip you to battle worry, train your fighting friends, and help you fight in faith. Let's review those tools.

Wisdom Over Worry

Count to 12

Jesus, I'm Hanging On to You

Seven Minutes of Silence

Search My Heart

Sort It Out

After-Action Review

Which of these tools have been helpful to you? Are there any that you might continue to use after the study? Circle them.

Prayer

God, thank You for being a safe place for me to run when I mess up. There may be times when I allow my worry to lead to panic and then a meltdown, but I can always turn around and run to You. Thank You for being so gracious and loving to me, even when I fail.

Today I come boldly to Your throne of grace and ask for Your help to _____.

Thank You for hearing my prayer. Instead of worrying, I will watch and wait for You to show up in this situation. In Jesus' name, Amen.

DAY 3: WATCHING OUT FOR EACH OTHER

Every other Wednesday, I meet with my friend Cindy. We worked together for many years, and she is truly a "heart sister" to me. My life is an open book for her, and her life is an open book for me. We care about each other's walk with Christ, and our time is spent building each other up and helping each other reach toward Christ in every area of our lives.

We don't always have our Bibles out. However, our time together is sixty minutes of rich spiritual conversation every other week over $1 coffee. Some weeks, I'm dragging the weight of the world in on my shoulders, and other weeks Cindy shows up weighed down. Whether we're celebrating or struggling, our goal is to hold each other accountable to walking with Christ during our difficulties and challenges.

I have several other "heart sisters" in my life who model Jesus' love for me, but I wanted to point out the strategic decision that Cindy and I have made to have a place and time to meet for accountability.

Choosing to open up our lives and allow people to celebrate with us, share concerns they have about us, or even correct us is hard. Most of us shy away from it. But you'll never hold on to your hard-fought victory over worry without someone in your life checking in on you with regularity.

Before we talk about what this kind of accountability looks like and why it's important, we're going to look into a situation where the Israelites on the western side of the Jordan responded to a questionable situation happening in the Israelite tribes on the eastern side.

Read Joshua 22:1-5. Which tribes did Joshua release to return home after the fighting was finished and the land allotted?

What did Joshua remind them to do in verse 5?

If you remember from earlier in our study, Moses gave the tribes of Reuben, Gad, and the half-tribe of Manasseh their land allotment on the eastern side of the Jordan. However, he told them that the fighting men in their tribes needed to cross the Jordan and fight with the other tribes until the entire campaign was

over. Now it was time for the fighting men from those eastern tribes to return home to their wives and families on the other side of the river. On their way home, however, they stop near the Jordan on the west side.

Read Joshua 22:10-14 and answer the following:

What did they build, and how was it described? (v. 10)

How did the rest of the Israelites react when they heard about the altar? (vv. 11-12)

Before waging war, what does the community of Israel do? (vv. 13-14)

The people of Reuben, Gad, and the half-tribe of Manasseh stopped to construct an altar of imposing size on the west side of the Jordan. We'll discover their motives for constructing the altar in just a bit, but it's clear that news of this altar is very disturbing for the Israelites, who are ready to make war. Just a short time ago, Joshua reminded the eastern tribes to follow and serve God alone (Joshua 22:5), and now these tribes have built an altar without the knowledge or approval of Joshua or any of the other leaders. In order to get to the bottom of what is going on, a delegation, including a member of the high priest's family and leaders from each tribe of Israel, set off to investigate.

Read Joshua 22:15-20. What does the delegation demand to know from the eastern tribes?

In their words we hear a desire to protect their covenant community from God's anger, and I think this is one of the shining moments of the entire Book of Joshua. Rather than just wishing the departing tribes *adios* and good luck, the people of Israel recognize that while the Jordan may split them geographically, they are one spiritually as a people.

Can you hear the desperation and pleading in the voices of the delegation? They essentially say, "Are you crazy? Don't you remember the thousands of people who died in the plague at Peor? Have you forgotten about what we saw when Achan was stoned? Don't be like this! Don't do this to us!"

The leader of the delegation is a priest named Phineas, whose zeal for upholding God's righteousness is recorded in Numbers 25. While the entire assembly was camped at Peor, the Israelite men had sexual relations with idol-worshiping Canaanite women. Not only that, the Israelite men went off with the women to offer sacrifices to the god Baal. As a result of their sin, a great plague began to kill thousands of people. But the plague stopped when Phineas, who had a heart for holiness and purity, killed an Israelite man and the Canaanite woman he had taken back to his tent—an act of defiant sin against God. The plague then ended because of Phineas's actions.

With this background in mind as I read the words of the delegation here in Joshua 22, I can imagine the intensity in Phineas's eyes as he and perhaps other leaders of the delegation fire off questions and a quick history recap for the eastern tribes. They had seen the sin of individuals affect the entire community before, and they did not want a repeat incident.

Can you think of a time when someone's bad decision or life choices created hardship or consequences for others in the family or community? If so, describe it briefly below:

In response to the delegation, the eastern tribes offer an explanation that calms the fears of the entire assembly.

Read Joshua 22:21-34, and mark each statement below with either a Y (yes) or an N (no):

_____ **1. The eastern tribes built the altar in rebellion to God.**

_____ **2. The altar was built to offer sacrifices.**

_____ **3. They wanted to build the altar so that the children of the western tribes wouldn't forget that the eastern tribes were part of God's covenant, too.**

_____ **4. They built the altar as a witness between the tribes, which represented their unity in the Lord their God.**

_____ **5. The people of Israel went ahead with their plans to wage war.**

Answers: 1. N, 2. N, 3. Y, 4. Y, 5. N

¹Dear brothers and sisters, if another believer is overcome by some sin, you who are godly should gently and humbly help that person back onto the right path. And be careful not to fall into the same temptation yourself. ²Share each other's burdens, and in this way obey the law of Christ. ³If you think you are too important to help someone, you are only fooling yourself. You are not that important.

(Galatians 6:1-3)

Once Phineas and the rest of the delegation realized that the altar named "Witness" was built to serve as a witness that they worshiped the same Lord (Joshua 22:34), the matter was settled. I admire the integrity and courage of the delegation. I know from experience that when there is uncertainty in a matter, it takes a lot of bravery to approach another believer and, in love and respect, ask questions about the veracity of their faith. I've been on both sides, and it's hard. Yet this is exactly what God calls us to do.

Read Galatians 6:1-3 in the margin and answer the following:

What are we to do when we see another believer struggling with sin?

What two attitudes should guide our approach in helping them?

What is the warning for us in verse 1?

What do we need to remember if we think we are too good or important to help those who are caught in sin?

During a past speaking engagement, I was just tired. I put on a big smile and took lots of deep breaths, but I was counting down the hours until I could return home. A good friend noticed my weariness and sent me a message the next day. She'd known that I had a busy run of speaking engagements, and she was concerned about my overall well-being.

This friend asked great questions about my schedule, times of rest, and stress levels, as well as my general spiritual and emotional health. She came from a place of great love and concern. Some of the questions were uncomfortable, because we don't like to justify our actions. But her questions were a precious opportunity for me to hold up my current condition and allow someone else to point out any blind spots that I was missing. At the end of our talk, I thanked her for being willing to reach out and ask the tough questions. She is someone that I can always count on as a true friend.

What has been your experience with someone who has shared a concern in love about an area of your life or decisions that you've made?

Have you ever approached someone in love to express your concern for them? If you have, how did it go? If you haven't, what are your concerns or worries about that type of conversation?

Renowned psychotherapist Dr. Harris Stratyner created the term "carefrontation"[8] as a treatment approach to help addicted individuals. Rather than direct confrontation, which can create defensiveness or shutdown, Dr. Stratyner advocates a carefrontation approach, which allows for a kinder, gentler road toward accountability and treatment. Mental health professionals, employers, coaches, teachers, and parents have borrowed Dr. Stratyner's original phrase, using it to set a new standard for engaging in difficult conversations.

While most of us hate confrontation, there are times when crucial conversations must happen, especially when you suspect that someone's life is sliding sideways into sin. How do we proceed with a carefrontation? Since I like food, the best way for me think about a carefrontation conversation is like a sandwich:

- A slice of love on top, affirming the person's value and the shared relationship.
- The meat of the concern in the middle, expressed with observations, not opinions.
- A slice of encouragement on the bottom, letting the other person know that you are for them—and that God is, too! Communicate that you want God's best for them in this situation.

Let's walk through the process together by creating a carefrontation sandwhich.

Extra Tool

Carefrontation Sandwhich

Is there a relationship in your life where a carefrontation might be needed? Take a moment to prepare by completing the carefrontation sandwhich on the following page. You can use these notes for your conversation.

Step 1: Slice of Love
Affirm the person's value and the relationship:

Step 2: Meat of concern
Express observations, not opinions:

Step 3: Slice of Encouragement
Communicate goodwill and share hope for the future:

Taking a proactive approach to carefrontation, we can give other people permission to care-front us, rather than confront us, on a regular or even scheduled basis. Proactive carefrontation is called accountability. Accountability can be hard to do because it forces us to confront our pride and self-centeredness routinely. Let's face it: we want to deal with that kind of business only when we have to, not to schedule it on our calendars! So, why do we want accountability? What are the benefits?

1. *We need to create positive tension to prevent the easy slide into selfish behavior.* When we think we can operate in life without answering to anyone, we're destined to make selfish and self-centered choices. Yet when we know that someone is going to ask us about our actions, just the thought of confessing to prideful or irresponsible behaviors is often enough to influence us away from such actions.

2. *We need someone that God can use to speak to us.* I believe that God can use anyone at anytime to speak to us. However, there is wisdom in surrounding ourselves with other believers who will point us toward God's plan for success, including studying and meditating on God's Word (see Joshua 1:8), pray for us, and speak to us using language that reflects God's character and heart.

3. *We need someone to help pull us out of the spiritual ditches that we'll end up in from time to time.* If your car slides into a ditch, you would think nothing of calling someone to help pull you out, right? Your car is too much of an investment for you to leave it there without getting help. Likewise, sometimes you may fall into a spiritual ditch and get stuck, and you are too precious to stay there. So if that happens, reach out to a trusted Christian friend and begin with the words, "I'm stuck, and I need help."

Who is someone in your life that you could invite into an accountability relationship?

What is something you could ask this person to help hold you accountable to do or not to do for the next thirty days after this study?

Apply It: Wisdom Wednesday

"Confess your sins to each other and pray for each other so that you may be healed. The earnest prayer of a righteous person has great power and produces wonderful results."

(James 5:16)

Prayer

God, give me a heart that desires accountability. It's not possible for me to win my battle over worry without the support and encouragement of my sisters in Christ. Give me the conviction and courage to seek out another woman who will encourage me and care-front me as I commit to fighting in faith and living in victory over worry. In Jesus' name, Amen.

DAY 4: YOUR CHOICE

We're down to the final two days of our time together. I hope that this journey through the Book of Joshua has been an eye-opening experience. Prior to this study, your familiarity with this book of the Bible may have been limited to the major stories, such as the crossing of the Jordan, the fall of Jericho, and the day that the sun stood still. Perhaps you had memorized Joshua 1:8 or some of the "be strong and courageous" verses but never explored the powerful connections between many of the book's events and those in the first five books of the Bible. Or perhaps you've studied the book previously but have come to an even deeper understanding of the truths within its pages, particularly as they relate to the worry battle. Whatever your experience has been, I pray it has been packed with liberating, life-giving truth and grace!

There are just a couple of chapters left for us to cover in the Book of Joshua. Since the battles have been fought and the inheritances have been given, these last two chapters could feel anticlimactic. Yet they contain some powerful final words spoken by Joshua to the assembly that also speak into our lives today.

Joshua 23 opens with the notice that a long time has passed since the end of the giving of the land inheritances. All of the nation of Israel has been summoned together. Now Joshua is an old man, and he is ready to pass along the mantle of leadership to the next generation with several important reminders.

Read Joshua 23:6-13, and fill in the blanks:

Make sure to do all that is _____ in the Book of the Law. (v. 6)

Do not mix with the _____ that remain among you. (v. 7)

Cling to _____ as you have done this day. (v. 8)

Since God _____ for you, no one will be able to stand against you. (vv. 9-10)

Be careful to _____ God. (v. 11)

If you _____ the inhabitants of the land, God will not drive them out; and they will entrap you. (vv. 12-13)

At this point, these instructions to the people might sound redundant. But in the words often attributed to writer Samuel Johnson, "People need to be reminded more often than they need to be instructed."[9] I've been a Christ-follower for a long time, and the only way to continuously go deeper with God is to stay faithful to the basic discipleship practices outlined in Joshua 1:8, which are to read the Bible, meditate on God's Word, and be obedient. Easy to remember, but hard to do!

In the next verses of Joshua 23, Joshua speaks to his audience in a manner fitting a grandmother or grandfather at the end of a very long and faithful life.

Read Joshua 23:14-16. What does Joshua say about God's track record regarding the promises made long ago?

God kept *all* of His promises. As D. L. Moody said, "God never made a promise that was too good to be true."[10] Joshua says to the people, "Deep in your hearts you know that every promise of the LORD your God has come true. Not a single one has failed!" (23:14). This statement is a preface to a foreshadowing and warning that Joshua rolls out in the following verses about what God will do if the people do not remain faithful.

The next and final chapter opens with a scene that mirrors Moses's covenant review in Deuteronomy. Joshua assembles all of the tribes of Israel in Shechem to revisit the covenant again. The town of Shechem is not only a city of refuge but also the place where God first made his covenant with Abraham (Genesis 12:6-7). It also is the place where Jacob stopped long ago to deal with some idols that his wife, Rachel, had stolen, as well as the place where Joseph's

bones are buried. So, this is a historic location to host Joshua's final address to the Israelites.

The final chapter begins with Joshua reminding the people of where they have come from and what they have been through.

Read Joshua 24:1-13, and answer the following:

Who did Terah, the father of Abraham, worship/serve? (v. 2)

Where did Jacob and his children go to live? (v. 4)

Who was sent to curse the Israelites but blessed them instead? (vv. 9-10)

What did God send to help drive out the inhabitants of the land? (v. 12)

Five hundred years of history is drilled down into thirteen verses! Maybe this recap is intentionally short, but it makes sense. People have limited recall, and too many details can cloud the memory. Yet the highlights are crucially important.

This gathering reminds me of family reunions. When I go to family reunions, I spend most of my time trying to learn and remember the names of the people I've meet that day, as well as the names of relatives who aren't present or are "dearly departed." So, it's incredibly helpful when a knowledgeable family matriarch or patriarch addresses the group.

At one family reunion, my grandmother's cousin asked us to divide up by family. Then she went around the room and told us about our ancestors. I loved hearing about my ancestors, but it also was so beneficial matching other ancestral relatives with the living members of their family who were at the reunion. Matching people to stories and connecting them all to us provided the needed context to affix them to my memory. This was especially valuable because in the hustle and bustle of life, it's easy to forget the roots of my people and how their life experiences are similar to my own.

This gathering of the Israelites shows us once again that they have made it a practice to rehearse their roots. As Joshua speaks to the people, he reminds them of God's mighty acts. Though he doesn't share all of the details, he does share some interesting moments, such as the reference in Joshua 24:12 (NIV)

On the Map

Turn to the map on page 11 and locate Shechem in the hill country of Ephraim of the tribe of Manasseh. Notice how the town is centrally located in the Promised Land. Many important events happened here in Israelite history.

to the hornets (in the New Living Translation: terror) that God used to drive out some of the inhabitants.

Can you recall other unique ways that God fought for the Israelites in the Book of Joshua? (*Hint*: Think about how they won some of their battles.)

We find the original reference to these hornets in Deuteronomy: "Moreover, the Lᴏʀᴅ your God will send the hornet among them until even the survivors who hide from you have perished" (7:20 NIV). Here in Deuteronomy 7, years before the Israelites begin their conquest of the Promised Land, the Lord gives an in-depth explanation as to how He will drive out the nations living there. In many ways, it is the preamble to the summary that we read in Joshua 24. In fact, much of what we read in Deuteronomy 7 is repeated by both Moses and Joshua throughout the Books of Deuteronomy and Joshua.

After Joshua's summary in Joshua 24:1-13, he throws down a gauntlet and gets personal with the people. Though they are a covenant community, each person must decide for themselves whom they will serve.

Read the challenge given in Joshua 24:14-15:

> ¹⁴ *"So fear the Lᴏʀᴅ and serve him wholeheartedly. Put away forever the idols your ancestors worshiped when they lived beyond the Euphrates River and in Egypt. Serve the Lᴏʀᴅ alone.* ¹⁵ *But if you refuse to serve the Lᴏʀᴅ, then choose today whom you will serve. Would you prefer the gods your ancestors served beyond the Euphrates? Or will it be the gods of the Amorites in whose land you now live? But as for me and my family, we will serve the Lᴏʀᴅ."*

What is Joshua telling the people to do?

1. Fear _____

2. _____ **Him wholeheartedly**

3. Put away _____

What choices are the people given?

The phrase "choose today whom you will serve" is often misunderstood as a choice between God and other gods in general. But read carefully and you'll see that it's not a question of either/or but a question of who, specifically. Notice that Joshua has already implored the people to serve God wholeheartedly and abandon worshiping other idols. He calls them to serve God only, and yet they have the free will to decide what they will do. So, if they do not want to serve God, Joshua tells them to take their pick of the gods that they could serve. It's in this moment that I imagine Joshua using a little sarcasm in his tone:

> My fellow Israelites, you've seen all that God has done for you, but if you don't want to serve Him, you've got a few other choices. Do you want to pick the unknown gods in Mesopotamia where our forefather Abraham was born? Remember, God rescued him from those gods so that he could be blessed by the true Almighty God. But hey, if you want to go back to those gods, it's your choice. Or, do you want to serve the god of the Amorites that our God trounced in battle? Friends, our mighty God has kicked their puny gods' behinds. But if you want to get cozy with those losers, go ahead. Like the song says, "It's your thang. Do what you want to do."

Maybe I went a little overboard, but I think Joshua really wanted the people to recognize that it's one thing to be a covenant community saying "yes" to God and another to make specific choices that honor God in their individual lives.

What woos you away from choosing God each day?

Choosing God is, well, a choice. No one can make this choice for you, and you can't hold anyone else responsible for what you choose.

Sometimes we let our feelings drive our faith. But the good news is that you don't have to *feel* like choosing God in order to say "yes" to God each day. Even when you don't feel like it, you can pick up your Bible or a Bible study and say, "God, I don't feel like reading, but I want to live in your victory. Help me to connect with you." On the days when I don't let my feelings keep me from saying "yes" to God, I end up feeling so much better after I study and pray! Througout the day, I'm able to honor God with my words and actions, think more clearly, stay calm, and sleep better. Ultimately, I enjoy life more when I choose God each day because I am reminded that God is with me and for me in every circumstance. I'm now able to say "yes" to bigger opportunities from God without letting fear or worry chase me away, and some of those opportunities have been pretty cool.

Our choice to follow God not only blesses us but also blesses others, too. Choosing God each day means that we're in position for God to use us to

Today's Takeaway

The reward of choosing God is the blessing of a rewarding life that fulfills us and blesses others.

influence our world in new ways. So, the reward of choosing God is the blessing of a rewarding life that fulfills us and blesses others.

Apply It: Temperature Check Thursday

During the first week of our study, you rated your level of worry in the important areas of your life. Without looking back at that exercise, complete this Wheel of Worry as it reflects your life now. Remember, you are not being graded or judged; just be honest for your own sake.

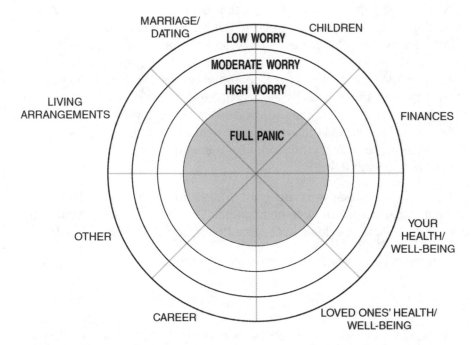

Now, flip back to page 33 and compare that Wheel of Worry with today's results.

Reflections:

1. What differences do you notice between the two Wheels of Worry? In what areas has your level of worry diminished?

2. To what do you attribute the reduction?

_____ **Change(s) in circumstances? If so, what change(s)?**

_____ **Practicing new tools? If so, what tools?**

_____ **Using specific spiritual disciplines? If so, which ones?**

3. If there is an area that has increased in worry, can you identify any contributing factors?

Don't worry if there are some stubborn places of worry in your life. The Israelites faced their own stubborn circumstances! Thankfully, God's victory is ours no matter what we're facing. Stay encouraged!

DAY 5: AMEN!

On this last day of our study, we're going to hear from the people of Israel as they respond to the challenge that Joshua has given them. Though our time together ends with a celebration of what God has done, is doing, and is yet to do in our lives, we will be leaving Joshua and the Israelites on somewhat of a somber note. As much as I want to celebrate the words of the people in Joshua 24, the rest of the Old Testament documents that the Israelites' sinful actions will speak louder than their passionate words on this occasion.

The same can be true for us, too. As we will see, it's important to avoid an all-talk-but-no-action reputation; but I'm thankful that because of Jesus, the burden of our covenant with God is not on us. Can I get an amen?

Let's see how the Israelite community responds to Joshua.

Read Joshua 24:16-18, and summarize the people's response to Joshua:

What is the final statement of the people in verse 18?

Most of the Book of Joshua is a narrative historical record without much dialogue. So the instances of dialogue stand out. We heard the Israelites respond in Joshua 1 when they affirmed their participation in the conquest of the Promised Land. We can't forget the loud shouts of the Israelites at Jericho in Joshua 6. Later, the community piped up when Joshua and the leaders made the ill-advised treaty with the Gibeonites in Joshua 9. In Joshua 17, the tribes of

Ephraim and Manasseh spoke up about their inheritances. And in Joshua 22, we read about the western tribes calling out the eastern tribes over a questionable memorial.

So, when I read the people's response to Joshua here in the final chapter, I want to applaud them because they sound as if they are responding in strong faith and conviction. After all, they've seen God do great and mighty things in their midst. They also are acknowledging how God has done great and mighty things prior to their time. Yet Joshua knows the true hearts of the people.

Read Joshua 24:19-20. How does Joshua describe God?

What does he say will happen to the people if they forsake God to follow other gods?

Joshua looks at the people and basically says, "Are you sure? You know that if you say you choose God, then you must choose Him each and every day. Is that the commitment you really want to make?"

Read Joshua 24:21-28 and answer the following:

When Joshua tells the people that they are the witnesses to their own decision to serve God, how do they respond? (v. 22)

What does Joshua tell the people to do, and how do they respond? (vv. 23-24)

What does Joshua do to confirm the people's decision? (v. 24)

What does the covenant agreement outline? (v. 25)

What will serve as the reminder of their agreement, and where is this reminder or witness placed? (vv. 26-27)

Let's upack this a bit. There's a reason Joshua is making such a forceful point here. Once upon a time long ago, Jacob and his family decided to flee from his father-in-law, Laban. As they were leaving, Jacob's wife Rachel stole some of her father's household idols. Laban tracked them down and searched for the idols in all of their possessions except one item belonging to Rachel, who deceived her father using a clever excuse that only a woman could use. (You can read her clever response in Genesis 31:34-35.) After Laban left, Jacob took the idols and buried them beneath a great tree by Shechem before they continued their journey (Genesis 35:1-4). Does that sound familiar? *Idols buried beneath a tree near Shechem.* The exact location where Jacob buried the idols is unknown because, as one commentator explains, Jacob didn't want anyone in his household to come back and try to find them.[11]

Joshua knows this story, and so his forceful command is framed by the historical significance of their location in Shechem. Not only that, but Joshua has seen enough to know the uncircumcised hearts of the Israelites. He knows there are people in the community who are still holding on to idols, even after everything they have seen and experienced. These people are living as part of the community but are not fully participating in the covenant. Even as their mouths are saying "yes," their hearts and lives are saying "no."

Read Isaiah 29:13 in the margin. How does God describe the difference between His people's hearts and words?

In Mark 7, Jesus confronts a group of religious leaders who question why Jesus' disciples don't follow the Jewish ritual of handwashing before a meal. The text describes this as a tradition that the religious leaders "cling to" as a check-the-box requirement for righteousness. In response, Jesus expands upon God's similar pronouncement in Isaiah.

Read Mark 7:6-8 in the margin. Why does Jesus say that they ignore God's commands?

Even as Joshua warns the people about punishment for idol worship, the people insist that they will serve and obey God. So Joshua makes a covenant with them, committing them to follow God's ways.

And so the Lord says,
*   "These people say*
*   they are mine.*
They honor me with
their lips,
*   but their hearts are*
*   far from me.*
And their worship of me
*   is nothing but*
*   man-made rules*
*   learned by rote."*
*   (Isaiah 29:13)*

---

[6] Jesus replied, "You hypocrites! Isaiah was right when he prophesied about you, for he wrote,

*   'These people honor*
*   me with their lips,*
*   but their hearts*
*   are far from me.*
[7] Their worship is a
farce,
*   for they teach*
*   man-made ideas*
*   as commands*
*   from God.'*

[8] For you ignore God's law and substitute your own tradition."
*   (Mark 7:6-8)*

As part of the old covenant outlined in the Old Testament, the Israelites must keep the Law in order to receive God's protection and blessing. Moses's address to the Israelites at the end of Deuteronomy details this agreement; and in Joshua's final address, he reminds the people of this agreement.

As followers of Jesus, we live under the new covenant. Because of Jesus' sacrificial death on the cross, we are forgiven when we sin against God. Unlike the old covenant of rules, the currency of the new covenant is God's grace and our faith. This covenant is sealed by our faith in Christ and His finished work on the cross, and it is eternal. The new covenant covers every area of our lives. But we also can make our own covenants with God—agreements about specific areas of our lives that we are committing to work on with the help of the Holy Spirit.

Would you consider entering into a covenant agreement with God regarding your worry battle? A covenant agreement related to worry isn't a sacred document, and it does not replace your personal relationship with Jesus Christ. It's simply an agreement that confirms your decision to continue taking steps in your battle against worry in a way that glorifies God and positions you for victory.

My friend, God has promised to give you peace, courage, and strength through the Holy Spirit who lives within you. He has promised to give you victory in every area of worry in your life. My prayer for you is that this agreement will help align your heart's desire with your actions—both now and in the future.

Are you ready?

COVENANT AGREEMENT

Acknowledging that God is my Source and Strength, and that my ability to fight worry comes only through the Holy Spirit who lives within me . . .

- I agree that I will immediately battle any worry that surfaces in my life and not allow weariness, compromise, apathy, or doubt to cause me to give up the battle.

- I agree that my fighting friends Peace, Courage, and Strength are gifts from God for me to train and develop in order to fight in faith and receive God's power over worry.

- I agree that I have been resourced with fighting tools so that I will never be without help to battle worry.

- I agree that my worry battle is for me to fight but that only God can provide the victory.

- I agree that there is never a worry battle too big that God cannot win for me.

- I agree that if I worry, panic, or have a meltdown, I will acknowledge my struggle as soon as I am able and call out to God for help.

- I agree that I will not condemn myself for worrying but will continue the fight, refusing to compromise for anything less than victory.

- I agree that God will receive the glory for any victories, and I will gladly share my story to encourage others to seek God for their own help.

Signed: _____ Date: _____

Apply It: Freedom Friday

Friend, I want to leave you with one final encouragement. As I mentioned in the introduction to this week's study, Christians often say the word *amen*, which means "so let it be."[12] As I think about everything that we've read, learned, and experienced together during our study, my deepest prayer is that your desire is not to lose any ground you've gained in your battle against worry. I hope that as various lessons continue to resonate in your heart, you will want to hold on to those lessons always.

So, as we close in prayer, I want you to emphasize the amen at the end to affirm your desire to continue along the road you've been traveling these past six weeks—a road to complete victory over worry through the grace and help of God. It has been a joy sharing this journey with you, and it is my privilege to offer this final prayer for you. I invite you to read it aloud, allowing it to be my benediction and blessing over you. And again, be sure to emphasize the "Amen!" at the end.

Prayer

God, thank You for walking with my friend, _____, through this experience. Whatever changes she has seen in her life and whatever victories she has experienced, I praise You for them. I pray that in the days ahead she will continue to fight in faith for the glory of Your name.

Remind _____ of Joshua's faithfulness when she feels those worry whispers creep in.

Remind _____ of Your promises to fight for her when circumstances feel like giant worry walls that block her way.

Remind _____ of Your promise to give her peace when she feels panicked and to pick her up after a meltdown with the whisper of Your word or the encouragement of a friend.

Most of all, God, never let _____ forget that victory over worry is hers as long as she is fighting with You.

Thank You, God, for giving us the power to live worry-free! While we may not be 100 percent there yet, we know that You will give us victory as we trust in You.

Amen!

Today's Takeaway

As long as I remember that God is with me and for me in every circumstance, I will always win over worry. Amen!

One of the key elements of choosing God's victory is to _____ _____ with others who will be a part of that journey.

Galatians 6:1-3—Share each other's burdens

Joshua 23:14-15—Joshua's reminder: God is faithful

Deep in our hearts we know that God has been _____ to us.

Each day we wake up with a choice…to _____ God instead of worry.

Joshua 24:14-15—"Choose today whom you will serve."

See page 206 for answers.

NOTES

Introduction to the Book of Joshua
1. Lane T. Dennis, et al., eds. ESV Study Bible, (Wheaton, IL: Crossway Books, 2008), 393.
2. Holman Reference Editorial Staff, Holman Illustrated Bible Dictionary for Kids (Nashville: B & H Publishing Group, 2010), 27.

Week 1
1. T. Borchard (2014). The Differences Between Normal Worry & General Anxiety Disorder. Psych Central. Retrieved on December 10, 2017, from https://psychcentral.com/blog/archives/2014/01/02/the-differences -between-normal-worry-general-anxiety-disorder/; accessed December 26, 2017.
2. Ari Ben-Menahem, Historical Encyclopedia of Natural and Mathematical Sciences, Vol. 1 (New York: Springer, 2009), 836.
3. Rego, Simon A, and Jennifer L Taitz. "Liberty Mutual Insurance Worry Less Report: A White Paper on the Prevalence of Worrying & Coping Mechanisms for Americans at Home or on the Road," released May 9, 2016, p. 3, https://www.libertymutualgroup.com/about-liberty-mutual-site/news-site/Documents/LMI%20 Worry%20Less%20White%20Paper%20FINAL.pdf; accessed February 1, 2018.
4. Timothy Lane, Living Without Worry: How to Replace Anxiety with Peace (The Good Book Company, 2015), 7.
5. Michael Moncur, "Quote from Chinese Proverbs," The Quotations Page, www.quotationspage.com/quote/34501 .html; accessed December 26, 2017.
6. Brett McKay, "Free Range Kids: Interview with 'America's Worst Mom' | Art of Manliness," The Art of Manliness, 5 July 2017, www.artofmanliness.com/2017/05/02/podcast-300-raise-free-range-kids/; accessed December 26, 2017.
7. Strong's Concordance, s.v. "Hoshea," http://biblehub.com/hebrew/1954.htm; accessed June 18, 2017.
8. Strong's Concordance, s.v. "Yehoshua," http://biblehub.com/hebrew/3091.htm; accessed June 18, 2017.
9. Sheila Walsh, The Shelter of God's Promises (Nashville: Thomas Nelson, 2011), 10.
10. Rick Warren, The Purpose Driven Life: What on Earth Am I Here For? Expanded Edition (Grand Rapids, MI: Zondervan, 2013), 92.
11. Russ Rankin, "Study: Bible Engagement in Churchgoers' Hearts, Not Always Practiced," www.lifeway.com /Article/research-survey-bible-engagement-churchgoers; accessed December 27, 2017.

Week 2
1. Henrietta C. Mears, What the Bible Is All About (Ventura, CA: Regal Books, 1983), 49.
2. J. Maxwell Miller and Gene M. Tucker, The Cambridge Bible Commentary on the New English Bible: The Book of Joshua 36–37 (New York: Cambridge University Press, 1974), 186.
3. John J. Bimson, The Compact Handbook of Old Testament Life (Bethany House Publishers, 1988), 23.
4. Lane et al., ESV Study Bible, 399.
5. Ronald F. Youngblood, Nelson's New Illustrated Bible Dictionary (Nashville, TN: Thomas Nelson, 1995), 306–307.
6. John Gill, "Commentary on Leviticus 26:41." John Gill's Exposition of the Whole Bible. https://www .studylight.org/commentaries/geb/leviticus-26.html; accessed December 27, 2017.
7. James I. Packer, et al., Daily Life in Bible Times (Nashville: Thomas Nelson, 1982), 125.
8. Youngblood, Nelson's New Illustrated Bible Dictionary, 647.
9. Bryant Wood. "The Walls of Jericho." Answers in Genesis, March 1, 1999, answersingenesis.org/archaeology /the-walls-of-jericho/; accessed December 27, 2017.
10. Robert Jamison, A. R. Fausset, and David Brown, Commentary, Joshua 2, https://www.blueletterbible.org /Comm/jfb/Jos/Jos_002.cfm?a=189001; accessed December 27, 2017.
11. Leander E. Keck, et al., The New Interpreter's Bible Commentary, Vol. 2, (Nashville: Abingdon Press, 2015), 47.
12. Bodie Hodge, "A Righteous Lie?" Answers in Genesis, 3 November 2008, https://answersingenesis.org /contradictions-in-the-bible/a-righteous-lie/; accessed December 27, 2017
13. Strong's Concordance, s.v. "Yada," http://biblehub.com/hebrew/3045.htm; accessed June 24, 2017.
14. "Commander of the Lord's Army," Ligonier Ministries http://www.ligonier.org/learn/devotionals/commander -lords-army/; accessed December 28, 2017.
15. Richard Foster, Celebration of Discipline: The Path to Spiritual Growth (New York, NY: HarperCollins Publishers, 1998), 98.
16. Ibid., 105–107.
17. Ibid., 101.
18. Steven J. Cole, "Psalm 46: Our Sufficient God," Psalms, https://bible.org/seriespage/psalm-46-our-sufficient -god; accessed December 28, 2017.

Week 3

1. "Qadash," The KJV Old Testament Hebrew Lexicon, Strong's 6942, http://www.biblestudytools.com/lexicons/hebrew/kjv/qadash.html; accessed December 28, 2017.
2. Mark Batterson, *All In: You Are One Decision Away from a Totally Different Life* (Grand Rapids, MI: Zondervan, 2013), 19.
3. Lane et al., *ESV Study Bible*, 405.
4. Melissa Spoelstra, *Numbers: Learning Contentment in a Culture of More* (Nashville: Abingdon Press, 2017), 146.
5. Ibid., 145.
6. David Kalas, *When Did God Become a Christian? Knowing God Through the Old and New Testaments* (Nashville: Abingdon Press, 2017), 104–105. Theodoret excerpt is from *Ancient Christian Commentary on Scripture*, Old Testament XIV (Downers Grove: InterVarsity, 2003), 2.
7. Melissa Spoelstra, "Digging Deeper Week 4: Shadows," from *Numbers: Learning Contentment in a Culture of More* (Nasvhille: Abingdon Press, 2017), http://www.abingdonwomen.com/files/uploads/Week4_Shadows.pdf. Excerpted commentary is from Roy Gane, *The NIV Application Commentary: Leviticus, Numbers* (Grand Rapids, MI: Zondervan, 1990), 622.
8. Norman L. Geisler and Thomas A. Howe, *The Big Book of Bible Difficulties: Clear and Concise Answers from Genesis to Revelation* (Grand Rapids, MI: Baker Books, 1992), 138–139.
9. Andy Stanley, North Point Community Church, "What Makes You Happy" video series, Part 1: *Nothing*, (40:20, beginning at 14:00 mark), August 15, 2015, http://northpoint.org/messages/what-makes-you-happy/nothing/; accessed December 28, 2017.
10. Dictionary.com, s.v. "Discourage," http://www.dictionary.com/browse/discouraged?s=t; accessed August 10, 2017.
11. Dictionary.com, s.v. "Dis," http://www.dictionary.com/browse/dis-; accessed August 10, 2017.
12. Lynn Cowell, *Make Your Move: Finding Unshakable Confidence Despite Your Fears and Failures* (Nashville, TN: Thomas Nelson, 2017), 16–17.
13. Jon Bloom, "Where Real Courage Comes From." Desiring God, June 19, 2015, www.desiringgod.org/articles/where-real-courage-comes-from; accessed December 28, 2017.
14. Batterson, *All In*, 122.
15. Seneca, Roman statesman, 5 BD-AD 65, https://www.brainyquote.com/quotes/lucius_annaeus_seneca_163577; accessed December 28, 2017.
16. Batterson, *All In*, 125.
17. *Blackie's Dictionary of Quotations* (Mumbai: Blackie & Son), 12.
18. "His Strength Is Perfect," Steven Curtis Chapman and Jerry Dean Salley Jr., Copyright ©1988 Sparrow Song (BMI) Greg Nelson Music (BMI) Universal Music—Brentwood Benson Songs (BMI) Universal Music—Brentwood Benson Tunes (SESAC) (Adm. At CapitolCMGPublishing.com). All rights reserved.
19. *Strong's Concordance*, s.v. "Endunamoó," http://biblehub.com/greek/1743.htm; accessed December 28, 2017.
20. *Strong's Concordance*, s.v. "En," http://biblehub.com/greek/1722.htm; accessed December 28, 2017.
21. *Strong's, Concordance*, s.v. "Dunamoó," from "Dunamis," http://biblehub.com/greek/1412.htm; accessed December 28, 2017.
22. D. L. Moody quotation from Pamela Rose Williams, "Top 25 Christian Quotes About Strength," *What Christians Want To Know* RSS, www.whatchristianswanttoknow.com/top-25-christian-quotes-about-strength/; accessed December 15, 2017.
23. Story from Leo Babauta in Michael Bungay Stanier, *The Coaching Habit: Say Less, Ask More & Change the Way You Lead Forever* (Toronto, ON: Box of Crayons Press, 2016), 19.
24. David T. Neal, Wendy Wood, and Jeffrey M. Quinn, "Habits—A Repeat Performance," *Association for Psychological Science* 15, no. 4 (August 1, 2006): 198–202.
25. *Strong's Concordance*, s.v. "Hagah," http://biblehub.com/hebrew/1897.htm; accessed December 28, 2017.
26. Robert L. Leahy, *The Worry Cure: Seven Steps to Stop Worry from Stopping You* (New York: Three Rivers Press, 2005), 109.
27. John Ortberg, *God Is Closer Than You Think* (Grand Rapids, MI: Zondervan, 2005), 92.
28. Tim Keller, *Prayer: Experiencing Awe and Intimacy with God* (New York, NY: Penguin Books/Random House, 2014), 146–148.
29. Priscilla Shirer, *Fervent: A Woman's Battle Plan for Serious, Specific and Strategic Prayer* (Nashville: B&H Publishing Group, 2015), 2.
30. Ortberg, *God Is Closer Than You Think*, 85.
31. Foster, *Celebration of Discipline*, 55.
32. Ibid.

33. Bill Bright, "How to Begin Your Fast," https://www.cru.org/us/en/train-and-grow/spiritual-growth/fasting/7-steps-to-fasting.2.html; accessed December 12, 2017.

Week 4

1. Chaim Herzog and Mordechai Gichon, *Battles of the Bible: A Military History of Ancient Israel* (New York, NY: Random House, 1978), 30.
2. Felicia R. Lee, "From Noah's Curse to Slavery's Rationale," *New York Times*, November 1, 2003, http://www.nytimes.com/2003/11/01/arts/from-noah-s-curse-to-slavery-s-rationale.html; accessed December 13, 2017.
3. Lane, *Living Without Worry: How to Replace Anxiety with Peace*, 30.
4. Craig Groeschel, *The Christian Atheist: Believing in God But Living As If He Doesn't Exist* (Grand Rapids, MI: Zondervan, 2010), 153.
5. Gleason L. Archer Jr., *New International Encyclopedia of Bible Difficulties* (Grand Rapids, MI: Zondervan 1982), 161.
6. Ibid., 161–162.
7. "Hurry," The Free Dictionary, https://www.thefreedictionary.com/hurry; accessed December 29, 2017.
8. Lysa TerKeurst, *The Best Yes: Making Wise Decisions in the Midst of Endless Demands* (Nashville: Nelson Books, 2014), 20.
9. Steven Furtick, *Sun Stand Still* (New York, NY: Multnomah, 2010), 8.
10. Ibid., 200–202.
11. Priscilla Shirer, *God Is Able* (Nashville: B&H Publishing Group, 2013), 94.
12. Jenni Catron, *Clout: Discover and Unleash Your God-Given Influence* (Nashville: Nelson Books, 2014), 11.
13. David Kalas, *When Did God Become a Christian? Knowing God Through the Old and New Testaments* (Nashville: Abingdon Press, 2017), 128.

Week 5

1. *Strong's Concordance*, s.v. "Oz," http://biblehub.com/hebrew/5797.htm; accessed December 13, 2017.
2. *Strong's Concordance*, s.v. "Azaz," http://biblehub.com/hebrew/5810.htm; accessed December 13, 2017.
3. *Strong's Concordance*, s.v. "Katharos," http://biblehub.com/greek/2513.htm; accessed December 13, 2017.
4. *Strong's Concordance*, s.v. "Horaó," http://biblehub.com/greek/3708.htm; accessed December 13, 2017.
5. Rodney Burton, *31 Keys to Possessing Your Promise* (CreateSpace Independent Publishing Platform, 2014), 11–96.
6. Andy Stanley, "Finding and Creating a Uniquely Better Product," presentation at Global Leadership Summit, WillowCreek Church, August 10, 2017.
7. Geisler and Howe, *The Big Book of Bible Difficulties*, 60.
8. "Oldest Gymnast," Guinness World Records, http://www.guinnessworldrecords.com/world-records/oldest-gymnast; accessed December 13, 2017.
9. "Hebron meaning," Abarim Publications, http://www.abarim-publications.com/Meaning/Hebron.html#.WfsaW44uqeo; accessed December 13, 2017.

Week 6

1. *Strong's Concordance*, s.v. "Amen," http://biblehub.com/str/greek/281.htm, accessed December 29, 2017.
2. *Strong's Concordance*, s.v. "Goral," http://biblehub.com/hebrew/1486.htm; accessed December 29, 2017.
3. Clinton E. Arnold, ed., *Zondervan Illustrated Bible Backgrounds Commentary* (Grand Rapids, MI: Zondervan, 2002), 230.
4. Sheila Walsh quotation in Christa Kinde, *Finding Freedom from Worry and Stress* (Nashville: Thomas Nelson, 2003), 11.
5. MacLaren Expositions on Holy Scripture, "Commentary on Joshua 20," *Bible Hub*; accessed July 12, 2017; http://biblehub.com/commentaries/joshua/20-1.htm; accessed December 13, 2017.
6. *Strong's Concordance*, s.v. "Ed," http://biblehub.com/hebrew/5707.htm; accessed December 29, 2017.
7. Lane et al., ESV *Study Bible*, 428.
8. "Carefrontation," Dr. Harris Stratyner website, January 21, 2013, http://www.drharrisstratyner.com/carefrontation/; accessed December 29, 2017.
9. Samuel Johnson quoted in Peter J. Schakel, *Imagination and the Arts in C. S. Lewis: Journeying to Narnia and Other Worlds* (Columbia, Missouri: University of Missouri Press, 2002), 87, note 18.
10. D. L. Moody quoted in *Every Day with Jesus: Treasures from the Greatest Christian Writers of All Time* (Brentwood, TN: Worthy Publishing, 2011), May 24.
11. John Wesley's Explanatory Notes, Genesis 35, Christianity.com website, https://www.christianity.com/bible/commentary.php?com=wes&b=1&c=35; accessed December 12, 2017.
12. *Strong's Concordance*, s.v. "Amen," http://biblehub.com/str/greek/281.htm;, accessed December 13, 2017.

VIDEO VIEWER GUIDE ANSWERS

Week 1
Insecurity
Personal
Provisional
Spiritual
with/for
What if/God if

Week 2
limitations
turn/God
knows
always/stands
brings
deserve
worry/pray
peace
Fix/God/wants

Week 3
security
commitment
empowers
Study
Meditate
Obey
God
hold/you

Week 4
priorities
fight
impossible
limit/tool
frantic
actionable/steps

Week 5
battle
plan/promises
Weariness
Compromise
Apathy
Doubt
drive/them/out
back/in
God's/best
old
others/blessed

Week 6
surround/ourselves
faithful
worship

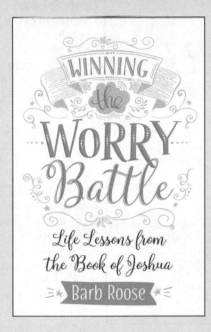

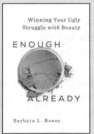
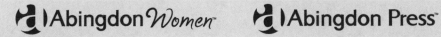 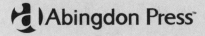

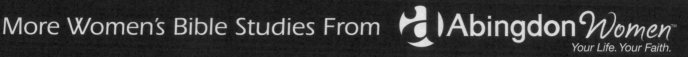
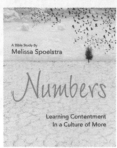

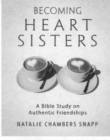
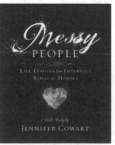